Divine Gossip and Tibetan Inroads

Divine Gossip opened at the Royal Shakespeare Co

'Two consumptive English writers, D H Lawrence
at the beginning of his, happen to be in Paris at the s
American poetaster, Harry Crosby, and his sculptre
which the three men have with death, and from thei
miraculously achieved through the love of a woman, Lowe has fashioned a sometimes
dazzling, sometimes incoherent, but always fascinating play.'

Francis King, *Sunday Telegraph*

Tibetan Inroads was first staged at the Royal Court Theatre, London in 1981. It was directed
by Bill Gaskill.

'Stephen Lowe's extraordinary new play is inspired by an epic clash of ideologies in 1950
when Chinese Marxism pierced the closed door of theocratic Tibet, where time had petrified
in a medieval stasis.'

Nicholas de Jongh, *Guardian*

Stephen Lowe

Stephen Lowe was born in 1947 in Nottingham. After graduating from Birmingham
University in 1969, he spent six years writing, and doing a variety of jobs. While working as a
shepherd in Yorkshire he was commissioned to write a play by Alan Ayckbourn and joined his
company at Scarborough as an actor. His plays include *Comic Pictures* (Scarborough, 1976),
Sally Ann Hallelujah Band (Nottingham Playhouse Theatre Roundabout, 1977), *Touched*
(Nottingham Playhouse, 1977; Royal Court Theatre, 1981; joint winner of the George Devine
Award), *The Ragged Trousered Philanthropists* (Joint Stock Theatre Company, 1978; Half
Moon, London, 1983), *Glasshouses* (Royal Court Theatre Upstairs, 1981), *Tibetan Inroads*
(Royal Court Theatre, 1981), *Moving Pictures* (Royal Court Theatre, 1981), *Seachange*
(Riverside Studios, 1984), *Keeping Body and Soul Together* (Royal Court Theatre Upstairs,
1984) and *Divine Gossip* (Royal Shakespeare Company's The Pit, 1988). He is Artistic
Director of the Meeting Ground Theatre, Nottingham, where he has directed his own plays
Desire (1986) and *Demon Lovers* (1987). His work for television includes *Shades* and *Cries
from a Watchtower* plus two films for Channel 4: *Unstable Elements* (1986) and *Ice Dance*
(due in 1989). He has also edited a volume of *Peace Plays* for Methuen, and a second volume
will be published in 1989.

DIVINE GOSSIP

&

TIBETAN INROADS

STEPHEN LOWE

Methuen Drama

A METHUEN NEW THEATRESCRIPT

First published in Great Britain as a paperback original in the Methuen New Theatrescript series in 1988 by Methuen Drama, Michelin House, 81 Fulham Road, London SW3 6RB Distributed in the United States of America by HEB Inc, 70 Court Street, Portsmouth, New Hampshire 03801.

Printed in Great Britain by Expression Printers Ltd, London N7 9DP

British Library Cataloguing in Publication Data
Lowe, Stephen, *1947-*
    Divine gossip; & Tibetan inroads.——(Methuen New Theatrescripts).
    I. Title
    822'914
    ISBN 0-413-61210-4

For Tanya

DIVINE GOSSIP

A Little Gossip

On the question of girls, George Orwell (formerly Eric Blair) once said that of all the girls he'd known before his wife, the one he loved best was a little trollop he picked up in a café in Paris. She was beautiful, had a figure like a boy, an Eton crop, and in every way was desirable. Anyway, he had a relationship with this girl for some time and came a point one day he came back to his room, and the paragon had decamped with everything he possessed.

Mabel Fierze, *Omnibus, 1970*

He wanders in the field picking flowers. I pray from my suntower . . . at suppertime in front of the fire I played the gramophone James Joyce reading aloud and after listening to it Lawrence said 'Yes, I thought so, a preacher, a Jesuit preacher who believes in the cross upside down.'

Shadows of the Sun, The Diaries of Harry Crosby

Frieda listened so often that weekend to Bessie Smith singing *Empty Bed Blues* that Lawrence broke the record over her head.

Keith Sagar, *Life of D H Lawrence*

Only a repetition of sun, sun, sun, not really a glowing symbol, more as a bewilderment and a narcotic.

D H Lawrence on Crosby's poems, *Collected Letters*

Pabst introduced me to the young woman of fascinating beauty who was sitting there, reading. Incredibly what this woman was reading was a translation of Schopenhauer's Essays . . . Years later, when I asked her why she had left films she told me bluntly she was bored.

Lotte H. Eisner, *On Louise Brooks*

Divine Gossip was premièred at the Royal Shakespeare Company's Pit Theatre on 12 October 1988, with the following cast:

ERIC	Linus Roache
ANGIE/LOUISE	Stella Gonet
BAILEY	Geoffrey Freshwater
HARRY	Nicholas Farrell
CARESSE	Pippa Guard
LAWRENCE/TED	Sean Baker
FRIEDA/SAM	Ann Mitchell
WALTER	Jim Hooper
OLD WOMAN	Deirdre Doone
OLD MAN	Arnold Yarrow
WAITERS	Emma Hitching
	Helen Sheals
	Philip Day
	Roger Tebb
	Mark Zingale

Directed by Barry Kyle
Designed by Gerard Howland
Choreographer Martin Duncan
Music Director Richard Brown
Magic consultant Ali Bongo
Stage Manager Jonathan Caldicot
DSM Rebecca Henson-Wilson
ASM Jayne Hedley-Boreham

This play is inspired by gossip, and, as such, is a complete fiction.

ACT ONE

As the audience enter:

Upstage, the shutters are closed, and unlit. Chairs stacked upside down on tables. Shadow figures of the waiters, dressed in black, sitting relaxed smoking.

White suited musicians move among them, as the small band assembles and begins to warm up. Eventually, one of them picks up an accordion and begins lazily to pick out the melody of 'J'Attendrai'. The pianist laughs, and joins in. The others slowly follow suit. The waiters begin, reluctantly, to move into action, setting out chairs, laying table clothes etc. A WAITER opens the mid-section of the shutters to reveal ANGIE.

Scene One:

L'Ange Noire

ANGIE, *a young woman, trapped in a shaft of light. It is raining heavily. She is dressed in an ill-fitting parody of the fashionable boyish look, trousers, jacket, boots far too big for her, her hair cut in the Eton crop. She shivers, then tilts her head listening to the music. She gradually makes her way into the cafe keeping a wary eye on the waiters – they do not deem to notice her. She half dances to the music and smiles nervously at the musicians.*

ANGIE (*sings*).
   J'attendrai le jour et le nuit
   j'attendrai toujours ton retour
   j'attendrai car l'oiseau qui s'en fuit
   vient chercher l'oubil dans son nid
   le temps passe et court en batant tristement
   dans ma coeur plus lourd et pourtant
   j'attendrai ton retour.

An elegant American couple: HARRY CROSBY, *late twenties and his wife,* CARESSE, *mid-thirties, enter. He stares down at a wilting bunch of flowers.*

BAILEY, *an obese, unstylish American enters, clutching a small bunch of flowers.*

HARRY. Damn. Damn. Damn. (*Grinning.*) You couldn't wave your magic wand over these, could you?

CARESSE. I can't work miracles, Harry.

HARRY. Jesus, what the hell's he going to think when we hand him these?

CARESSE. That we've been listening to gossip. And haven't we?

A WAITER takes her coat. ANGIE stares admiringly at her dress. A WAITER moves up to him.

HARRY. Champagne! Et les huitres!

The band begin an American waltz.

CARESSE. Dance with me.

HARRY. I have to meet my black angel first.

He moves to a table. CARESSE sighs, and sways to the music. ANGIE imitates her. BAILEY watches, and tentatively holds the flowers out until he sees CARESSE already has a bunch. ANGIE holds out a hand.

BAILEY. Sorry. I could never make it with a gal who looked like my brother. I hate the skinny little bastard.

ANGIE. Comment?

BAILEY. Excuse moi. I so little expected to meet anybody French in Paris, I clean forgot my phrase book. Get out of the way, honey. I've paid for the floor show. My only joy in life is watching.

A WAITER pops champagne. BAILEY clutches his stomach as though shot. He sits at a table. ANGIE, apparently concerned sits by him.

BAILEY. That bastard is out to kill me. What does she see in him?

A WAITER brings him a glass of milk. HARRY takes out a small phial and from it a black pill. The WAITER watches him.

HARRY. Mon Ange Noir.

CARESSE. Do you really need it?

HARRY. I don't need her. She doesn't need me. But we desire each other.

CARESSE. Are the two things so different?

HARRY. Need succumbs to weakness. Desire demands courage.

CARESSE. You fear her then? (*Pause.*) Do you have to be so public?

HARRY. Opium is the religion of the poet. (*He looks at the* WAITER.) Communist or Catholic? You ought to get a faith that leads you somewhere. (*Takes the pill.*)

The WAITER *moves away.*

HARRY (*grins*). Caresse, I miss you.

CARESSE. But I'm always here.

She sits, her arm around him.

BAILEY (*seeing this*). Caresse. Who'd have figured loving a woman called Caresse could cause such a deep pain in the pit?

ANGIE. Caresse? Desirez-vous une caresse?

BAILEY. Like hell I do.

She reaches towards him. He shudders convulsively. She stops, then slowly sniffs the air.

BAILEY (*amused*). What chance Esperanto when the language of flatulence is already universal?

He takes out a cigar. A WAITER moves in with a lighted taper. CARESSE eats the oysters putting the shells to her mouth.

BAILEY (*wafting smoke*). I see her. But it's always through a haze. She doesn't even know I'm alive. I can confess to you, because you can't understand. The whole thing is not without a certain pleasure you see.

He begins to talk/sing 'My Suppressed Desire'.

There she goes my suppressed desire
No one knows my suppressed desire
I supposed you'd like to know who she is?

Here's a reason, it's plain to see
She just doesn't belong to me

Now you know why
She's my suppressed desire.

If you have someone
you love secretly
That's the reason enough
in all you see

I'm so happy
when I retire
My heart feels
like a blazing fire
while I'm dreaming about
my suppressed desire.

Boy she likes to eat and how
I could buy her a steak right now
If only I could get a break
I'd buy her a cow
She's my suppressed desire.

(*Spoken.*) It's nice to tell somebody. As long as they don't understand you. Allez.(*He waves her away.*) I am expecting a guest. (*To the* WAITER.) Bring me the plate of the day.

ANGIE *rises, meets the cold stare of a waiter, and moves back outside, but still hovering. Outside, an old* FRENCH COUPLE *stand looking yearningly in.*

HARRY. He may not come in this rain.(*Stretches out his arms.*) O, Ra, O Sungod! Don't betray your faithful acolyte! Don't tell me you're only present in the deserts. Let me see your face. I have faith. (*Turning back.*) He won't show. I know he won't.

ERIC *hovers by the door listening.*

CARESSE. He'll come.

HARRY. How can you be so sure?

CARESSE. You ever know a writer turn down a meal with a publisher?

He smiles.

CARESSE. Besides, what if he doesn't?

HARRY. You're not serious?

CARESSE. You're behaving like you did on our first date, Harry. Don't make me jealous. (*Quietly.*) Leastways, not over a dying man.

HARRY *looks at her startled. A thin young man,* ERIC *enters, he wears a shabby sports coat and flannels and clutches a wad of sodden manuscripts.* HARRY *turns, still startled and his flowers are crushed to pieces.*

ERIC. Oh, pardon. Pardon.

HARRY *stares at the flowers, as the last petals fall off. A* WAITER *with a tray watches them.*

ERIC (*kneeling down to pick them up*). Oh, God, I'm awfully sorry.

HARRY. They were dying anyway. (*Smiles.*) You just delivered the coup de grace. A pun.

ERIC. Mr Bailey?

HARRY. Never heard of him.

CARESSE. Over there.

As ERIC *stands he collides with the* Waiter *– food and manuscripts go everywhere.*

HARRY. I think I'd better get out of the line of fire.

BAILEY. I fear that was your repast.

ERIC. Sorry.

ERIC *and the* WAITER *scramble about on the floor.*

BAILEY. No need to eat your dinner off the floor, Mr Blair. It's most uncivilised.

ERIC. I wasn't hungry, anyway.

BAILEY. You say that as though you eat every day. Encore. (*To the* WAITER.) And a cognac.

BAILEY *watches* CARESSE *as she kisses* HARRY *lightly.* BAILEY *sighs.* ERIC *still on his knees, turns, confused to see what is happening.*

BAILEY. You know Harry Crosby, the black sheep of the Morgan Banking family? Calls himself a poet. His wife, Caresse, is a sculptor. They run Black Sun Press. (ERIC *shakes his head.*) Don't consort with the cognoscenti?

ERIC. Not really. I once ate with James Joyce. In the same restaurant. I drank pernod.

BAILEY. Crosby publishes him.

ERIC *looks at him with renewed interest.*

BAILEY. He's very esoteric. No use to you I fear, unless you fancy writing up your Burmese days à la mode de Baudelaire.

ERIC. I don't intend to write about Burma. (*Pause.*) And I've never read Baudelaire.

BAILEY. Very wise, Mr Blair. All he does is provide my compatriots with an aesthetic excuse for excess. Not that they need encouragement.

ERIC. If you feel like that why bother coming over?

BAILEY (*sighs*). Right now our readers have a taste for a touch of surrogate decadence. It gives us Americans a false sense of maturity. You've read the novels of Henry James, I suppose?

ERIC. Not exactly.

He turns to pick up the last sheets, to come face to face with the OLD MAN *who grins, holds up the flowers he has been collecting and scurries back outside. The* OLD MAN *presents them to the* WOMAN.

BAILEY. What are you doing here, Mr Blair? I know this is laughingly called the Latin Quarter but it is hardly a home for a classical scholar.

ERIC (*pause*). Are you going to publish me?

BAILEY. I'm an agent not a publisher. I don't own the brothel. All I do is help you tart up your wares.

ERIC. I'm a writer, not a whore.

BAILEY. Mea culpa.

ERIC. What?

BAILEY. Sit down, please.

ERIC (*desperately wiping the food stains off his writings*). I brought you some more . . . I think they're better. They're ... the rain's ... I'll dry them out and post them to you. What do you think of what I sent you?

BAILEY. You're a wreck. Most writers are. But you are salvageable. As long as you don't let your life poison your art.

ERIC. What does that mean?

BAILEY. Mr Blair, let's lay the cards on the table. (*He begins to clear the table;* ERIC *looks as though he is expecting a trick. The food arrives.*) You write very powerfully, very powerfully indeed, but folk won't buy work that puts them off their dinner. Bon appetit!

A shaft of sunlight. The band respond to it.

Outside LAWRENCE *turns illuminated in a rainbow. He moves towards the restaurant. The* OLD WOMAN *holds out the flowers and a begging hand at him.* ANGIE *also holds out a hand, tentatively. He ignores her.* LAWRENCE *closes his umbrella, and steps inside.* ANGIE *carefully follows him, and hovers by the door. He stands by* HARRY.

HARRY (*rises unaware. Sings*).
Keep your sunny side up!
(*Sways, turns.*) Lawrence! (*Pause.*) Harry Crosby.

LAWRENCE. You look as if you're about to burst into song.

HARRY. No chance of that.

LAWRENCE (*smiling*). Thank God. I hate music, except hymns. And even those incite me to argument.

HARRY. It's a pleasure and a privilege to meet you, sir.

HARRY. Let me take that. (*Gives umbrella to* WAITER.)

LAWRENCE. Caresse? (*Takes her hand. Suddenly shivers.*) Can I sit down?

CARESSE. Please.

LAWRENCE. Cities exhaust me. In the country, we feed off the land, whilst the city seems to feed off me. Especially at night. The electric supply is wired into me. Whenever the lights come on, I feel an irresistible desire to lie down.

He closes his eyes. HARRY *stands nervously behind him.* CARESSE *rises, and embraces him tenderly.* BAILEY *groans.*ERIC *sniffs his meal, and looks up.*

BAILEY. Something the matter?

ERIC. Nothing, it's ... Is this fresh?

BAILEY. I never eat when I'm abroad.

ERIC *stares at him, and sniffs.*

BAILEY (*defeated*). Should have known I'd never hide it from one of the rose-growing class. (*Pause.*) A personal problem. (*Pause.*) You can't imagine what havoc it plays with one's intimate relationships. That's why I look to art for some consolation. And that I share, not the wind but the desire, with a large percentage of our readership.

ERIC (*smiling*). Perhaps I could write a best seller on flatulence.

BAILEY (*while puffing cigar smoke over the meal*). There you go again. Like some eighteenth century lord insisting we should all throw away our perfumed hankies and sniff the open sewers for the sake of our souls. Why? We all know we are standing in a cesspool. That's why we created both lace and perfume in the first place, to waft us away to Elysium while our shoes shuffle in the shit. It's no coincidence that Paris, the city of artists, is the home of both scent and sensibility.

ERIC. Tell Rabelais.

BAILEY. Sure, genius can turn even a fart into high art. Le Petomane, in Paris, before the war, he transformed my particular cri de coeur into melodious form, lifted the wind instrument to sublime levels. I still weep at his recording of the Ode to Joy. He understood that all art, artists, perhaps all life itself is sick, at the fundament. That we start incontinent and may end the same way, with largely wobbles in between, but the trick of art is it deals in the 'imaginings' of health, in pretend, it is the warm lie of lilacs and heavily laundered sheets. It is an essential illusion that fulfils our needs.

ERIC. I don't think that – (*The smoke sets off his cough.*)

BAILEY. OK?

LAWRENCE (*looking up*). Better.

CARESSE. You must both come stay at the Moulin de Soleil. That'll restore you. Rousseau lived there, and before that, Cagliostro worked his spells out by the sacred pool.

HARRY. I perform my sun rituals out there now.

LAWRENCE. Really? (*Pause.*) I must go south, as soon as I've got a publisher for a popular edition of my *Lady Chatterley*. Makes me feel like a pimp, all this. Not that Lady C. minds. She knows she's a whore. It's only me who's haunted by dreams of ancient priestesses. Frieda says I'm poisoned with the delusion of purity.

ERIC (*recovering*). But, surely, you believe that truth lies at the very heart?

BAILEY. Artists don't deal in truth, but dreams and nightmares. You give us hell, but where on earth is your heaven?

HARRY. Champagne?

LAWRENCE. Tea?

HARRY. I doubt it.

BAILEY. Where is your love? Or are you beyond such paltry desires?

LAWRENCE. Frieda normally packs me up with a flask. It's the only modern invention I approve of.

CARESSE. Is she still in Trieste?

LAWRENCE. Is it common knowledge? (*Pause.*) Water.

ERIC (*pause*). *The Sea God* is all love.

BAILEY. No, it's not. It's about sex. Sex runs through your sea like some stinking sewer. I have to be frank with you. You read like a coroner's report on the corpse of love, without us ever having seen the living flesh.

ERIC *pushes his food away.*

HARRY. Would you care to eat, Mr Lawrence?

LAWRENCE. Do you know Sylvia Beach?

CARESSE. Somewhat.

LAWRENCE. Thought she might like to make a fortune having thrown so much away publishing that crazy Jesuit, Joyce. She looked at My Lady like I'd slipped her some Parisienne postcards. Is she terrified of sex?

HARRY. I doubt she knows much about it.

LAWRENCE (*amused*). Who does really?

CARESSE. We rather thought you did.

LAWRENCE. My Lady does. I learnt all I know from her.

HARRY. Give him the present.

She rummages in her bag.

ERIC. You are saying my work is hopeless.

BAILEY. No, I'm not, I'm saying think of us, the reader, we live by your imagination. We don't ask that what you give us be true, only that it's an image of what we don't possess.

She holds out a parcel.

CARESSE. *The Sun* by D H Lawrence.

HARRY. Published by Black Sun Press. Can you feel the heat rising from it?

CARESSE. Open it. Please.

LAWRENCE *begins to gingerly unwrap it.* CARESSE *puts her arm around the nervous* HARRY. BAILEY *watches them.*

BAILEY. Come on Eric, give me the image of the unattainable. Love.

ERIC *turns round to see what he is looking at.* ANGIE *steps into his line of vision, and begins dancing gently.*

ERIC. I don't know anything about love.

BAILEY. So you spit on the image of it. Practise an art of spite. (*Pause.*) I take it there was not a whole lot of finesse in relationships in the Far East?

ERIC. Only husband hunters, and whores, like her. The Mary Magdalenes of Mandalay.

BAILEY. Does that render them incapable of love? (*Pause: seeing* ANGIE.) Take her. Does being a whore deprive her of the possibility of love and loving?

ERIC. Perhaps.

BAILEY. Couldn't there be an occasional real flicker of warmth buried among the shit of her well rehearsed gestures? (*She smiles at him.*) Mam'selle. (*Rises.*) Isn't she beautiful? Like an angel.

ERIC. Angels in Paris all have hearts of stone.

BAILEY. Then bring them to life, Pygmalion.

ANGIE. Angel? C'est moi. Je m'appelle Angeline.

BAILEY. What she say?

ERIC. She's taken the part you've offered her.

BAILEY. Or maybe I just divined the truth? Ask her to sit. Please.

ERIC *hesitates. She sees the manuscripts.*

ANGIE. Etes-vous des auteurs?

ERIC. Moi. Oui.

ANGIE. Bravo!

BAILEY. You see yourself as above desire. Maybe you simply daren't risk it.

ANGIE. Desire. Moi, je desire . . .

ERIC. Comment?

ANGIE. Je desire . . . apprendre . . . quel est le mot?

ERIC. To learn.

ANGIE. To learn . . . Americain.

BAILEY. God I wish half of New York had the same ambition.

She stares at him.

BAILEY. Offer her a glass of wine.

ERIC. Voulez-vous desirer un verre de vin?

She nods, politely. ERIC *pours her a drink.*

BAILEY. Out of the sewers of the streets a frail rose grows. Our little Paris Mam'selle has been the source of inspiration for countless works of art.

He gives her his bunch of flowers.

ANGIE. Merci, monsieur.

BAILEY. La Dame aux Camelias.(*Takes her hand: to* ERIC.) Feel.

ERIC *reluctantly takes her hand.*

BAILEY. Tell her, Mimi, your tiny hand is frozen. Then tell me, write me the story. It'll be money well invested. (*He lays out money on the table.*) The meal, including dessert, is on me. (*Pause.*) Or do you prefer to starve? Try one night of heaven. Tomorrow you can return to the security of hell. You have to risk something for your art. I want to read it in every loving detail. Good bye, Eric.

He shakes his hand.

ERIC. Are you taking me?

BAILEY. Let's wait and see. (*Kisses her hand.*) Au'voir, mam'selle.

He moves towards the CROSBYS.

ANGIE. Il est parti?

ERIC. Oui.

ANGIE. Et vous, aussi? Vous allez partir?

ERIC. No. Not yet.

BAILEY *hovers over* LAWRENCE. HARRY *gives him a look.*

BAILEY. Harry Crosby.

HARRY. Yes.

BAILEY. L I Bailey. (*Pause.*) We met at a party at Kay Boyle's last fall.

HARRY (*not remembering*). Ah, yes.

CARESSE. How are you, Mr Bailey?

BAILEY. Stops and starts. You know.

She nods.

How's Black Sun press weathering?

CARESSE. The same.

BAILEY. The same what?

CARESSE. Stops and starts.

BAILEY. Right.

ERIC. Would you care to eat? Mangez?

ANGIE. Non. Merci.

ERIC. J'ai fini.

ANGIE. Eh bien . . . (*Eats ravenously.*)

ERIC. I'll get you a plate. Garçon!

The WAITER *takes no notice.* LAWRENCE *looks up at* BAILEY *but* HARRY *does not make an introduction.* LAWRENCE *continues reading.* HARRY *doesn't take his eyes off* LAWRENCE.

BAILEY. Well, I'd better be starting again.

CARESSE *nods. She looks away.*

BAILEY. Au'voir.

He groans, and turns away.

HARRY. Creep.

LAWRENCE *looks up and sniffs.*

HARRY (*nervously*). You don't like it?

LAWRENCE. No, no, it's not that, it's just . . . no, it's beautiful.

HARRY *sighs with relief.*

CARESSE. Harry will be able to sleep tonight.

LAWRENCE (*smiles*). I think I need a little fresh air.

CARESSE. It has turned stuffy in here.

HARRY. Let's go on to Pruniere's and celebrate.

LAWRENCE. I need to get back to the hotel.

HARRY (*disappointed*). Sure. You rest here a minute. I'll get my car and we'll drive you round.

LAWRENCE. Please, don't bother.

HARRY. It's a pleasure. I've got to go that way anyway.

CARESSE. Why?

HARRY. I'll meet up with you later at Dingo's.

CARESSE. Where are you going?

HARRY. Hem and Bob McAlmon are back from Pamplona. You wouldn't enjoy it. Only talk of bullfights.

LAWRENCE *looks at her.*

CARESSE (*quietly*). He's quite right. I wouldn't.

HARRY. Garçon! (*Rises. The* WAITER *approaches.*) Le parapluie!

ERIC. Garçon! (*The* WAITER *moves away. Furious.*) Excuse me a moment.

ANGIE *is too busy to notice.* ERIC *moves off.* HARRY *watches* ANGIE.

CARESSE. You really must come and stay with us.

HARRY. We have our own race track . . . mind you, it's only for donkeys.

CARESSE. And Clytoris.

LAWRENCE. Clytoris?

CARESSE. She's our whippet.

LAWRENCE. Bit of an unusual name, isn't it?

CARESSE. More a nickname really. We call her that because Harry can never find her at night.

Silence. Then LAWRENCE *bursts out laughing. It starts a coughing fit, but he waves them back and takes a sip of water.*

HARRY (*grinning*). You must forgive Caresse. She has a coarse sense of humour. She's from New York.

CARESSE. But I'm struggling to become cultured. That's why I spell her name with a Y . . . C . . . L . . . Y . . T . . . I feel that's so much more refined.

LAWRENCE. Sir Richard Burton did that with cunt, you know.

CARESSE (*pause*). Did he?

HARRY. Where does he put the Y in cunt?

LAWRENCE. In his version of the *Arabian Nights*.

HARRY. Ah.

The WAITER *hands* HARRY *the umbrella.* ANGIE *picks up the money, and makes for the door.* HARRY *blocks her way.*

HARRY. You should at least leave a tip.

ANGIE. Pardon, monsieur, je ne parle pas l'Americain.

HARRY. Donnez un pourboire. Pour le pauvre garçon.

ERIC *approaches with a plate. The* WAITER *hovers nearby.*

CARESSE. What is it, Harry?

ERIC. Il y'a un problème?

HARRY. Your little friend's aiming to leave you to do the washing up.

ANGIE *puts the money on the plate.*

ERIC (*pauses*). There must be some misunderstanding.

HARRY. Of course. The American abroad. Nous sommes fous, n'est-ce pas?

He steps to one side, and ANGIE *runs out. The* WAITER *takes the plate off the stunned* ERIC. *Too late he reaches for it, then runs out.*

LAWRENCE. What's going on?

HARRY (*laughs*). L'amour.

LAWRENCE. Is there still light?

HARRY. A little.

CARESSE. Promise you'll come?

LAWRENCE. I must find someone for my Lady.

CARESSE. Well, we normally only deal in limited editions, but (*Hesitates.*) c'est possible.

LAWRENCE (*pause*). I suppose I'll have to come. If only to find out what you've called your donkeys.

CARESSE *laughs.*

HARRY (*to himself*). It's raining again. How dare it?

He opens the umbrella for LAWRENCE *and they leave.* CARESSE's *smile fades. She lights a cigarette. The* WAITERS *close the shutters, leaving only the mid-section open, and transform the scene. As they do so they sing* Rain.

WAITERS.
Rain let us huddle while the rain
pitter patters on the pane
and we're alone

our chance to while away
a dreamy afternoon
a lovely peaceful afternoon
no one can see us

Rain it's so cosy in the rain
there's no reason to complain
if I'm with you

CARESSE.
to hold her hand, and then
it's ten to one you'll kiss her,
in the rain,
you'll kiss her in the rain.

They place a large covered dish in front of her, but leave it unopened.

CARESSE. Who is it tonight, Harry? Is it the Shadow or the Sorceress? Don't kiss her in the street, Harry. Take her inside. Close the shutters. For me.

CARESSE *remains, smoking.*

Scene Two

Une Nuit Blanche

ERIC's *cheap hotel room, at 6 Rue de Pot de Fer. A small, single bed. Table with notes. The sound of lovemaking, even the* WAITERS *stop for a beat to listen. A shutter door opens.* ANGIE *stands in it. She slowly steps into the room.* ERIC *appears behind her. He closes the door.*

ANGIE (*eventually sighs*). Vous n'etes pas riche.

ERIC *laughs bitterly, coughs.*

ANGIE. Les voisins sont jolis.

ERIC (*to himself*). Is that the sound of joy?

ANGIE. Comment?

ERIC. Et toi? Es-tu une fille de joie?

ANGIE (*pauses*). Je suis actrice.

ERIC. Like I'm a writer.

He turns away to take off his wet coat. She does the same and begins to unbutton her shirt.

ERIC (*turning back*). There's no need . . .

ANGIE. Need?

ERIC. Besoin.

ANGIE (*frowns*). Vous n'avez pas the . . . need?

Silence. He lights a cigarette, and coughs.

ERIC. No money. Pas d'argent. Je suis professeur d'anglais. Mais . . . j'ai besoin d'etudiants.

ANGIE. Vous . . . learn . . . aux etudiants . . . Americain?

ERIC. 'I guess so.' (*Nods.*)

ANGIE (*eagerly*). J'ai besoin de . . . learn . . . Americain.

ERIC. Pourquoi?

ANGIE (*with effort*). Les films. (*Pause.*) Les films parlants maintenant.

ERIC. Talkies.

ANGIE (*smiling*). Mais oui. Talkies. America. Actrice. Moi.

ERIC smiles.

ANGIE (*frowns*). C'est amusant?

ERIC shakes his head.

ANGIE. Vous . . . learn . . . moi?

He looks quietly at her.

ANGIE. Pas d'argent. Money?

ERIC. Money.

ANGIE. No money. Mais . . . (*She smiles.*)

ERIC. Les leçons d'amour?

She grins.

ERIC. Oh, Professor Higgins. What have you done to us?

ANGIE. Comment?

She moves towards him. He stops her with a tentative gesture.

ANGIE. Vous ne me desirez pas?

ERIC. I always have. Even when I made you crawl through the monsoon in your white temple dress. Even when you'd cheated me. Every time I write the mud of Mandalay stains my white sheet. I don't know that I can go through that again. (*Shivers.*)

ANGIE. Etes-vous chaud?

He shakes his head.

ANGIE (*she takes his hand*). Comment s'appele la main en Americaine?

ERIC (*pauses*). La main s'appelle the hand.

ANGIE. De hand. Et les doigts?

ERIC. The fingers.

ANGIE. La maine, de hand, les doigs, de fingers. Je pense que je suis le bon ecolier. J'ai gagné deux mots d'Americaine. (*Raises his hand to her lips.*) Comment s'appele les lippes?

ERIC. La même. The same word.

ANGIE. Nous avons beaucoup en commun. (*Licks his fingers.*) La main. De hand. Les doigts. Fingers, Les lippes. La même. La langue?

ERIC. Tongue.

ANGIE. Tongue (*Places his hand on her breast.*) Les seins?

ERIC. Breasts.

ANGIE. Breasts. (*Moves his hand down.*) Le ventre?

ERIC (*confused*). Whose lesson is this?

ANGIE. Le mot?

ERIC. Stomach. Belly.

ANGIE. Belly. Belle. (*Moves his hand to her cunt.*) L'enfoire. (*Silence.*) Comment s'appelez l'enfoire? Le chat?

ERIC. It's not a word you're likely to use much in the talkies.

ANGIE. Le mot.

ERIC. Vagina. No. Cunt. Cunt.

ANGIE. Cunt. (*Moves in closer, placing his hand behind her*) La lune?

ERIC. Behind. Arse. Arse.

ANGIE (*whispers*). Arse.

She touches his trousers.

ANGIE. Eh voici . . . ? La bitte? (*Smiles.*) La verge?

ERIC. Il y a beaucoup de noms.

ANGIE. Tous. Tous.

ERIC. Penis. Prick. Cock.

ANGIE. What you call it?

ERIC. I never call it. I don't know. Cock. I call it cock.

ANGIE. Le coq. (*As ERIC shivers.*) Vous etes froid?

ERIC *suddenly pulls her back on top of him onto the bed.*

ANGIE. Que faisons-nous maintenant?

ERIC. You know what we are doing.

ANGIE. Le mot. Baise. Baise.

ERIC. We make love. No. How do you know? How would you ever know? We fuck. We fuck.

ANGIE. Fuck. Breast. Arse. Hand. Cock. Cunt. You, men,
you ... love ... the words, yes?

ERIC. Yes, oh, yes, oh god, yes.

She quietly murmurs the litany of her lesson as they make love.

The shutter door opens. A white light cuts across the edge of the bed. LAWRENCE *stands there.*

LAWRENCE *(murmuring in dialect)*. 'What is cunt?' she said. 'An doesn't ter know? Cunt!
It's thee down there; an' what I get when I'm i'side thee, and what tha gets when I'm inside
thee; it's all on't.' 'All on't' she teased. 'Cunt! It's like fuck then.' 'Nay nay! Fuck's only
what you do. Animals fuck. But cunt's a lot more than that. It's thee, dost see: and th'art a
lot besides an animal, aren't ter? – even ter fuck? Cunt! Eh, that's the beauty o' thee lass!'
Oh, my Lady. Oh, Frieda. Frieda.

ERIC. Angeline. My angel.

LAWRENCE *(suddenly angry)*. Why the hell does your lover have to be called Angelo? And
you go to fuck in Trieste. Triste. How sad. I may no longer have the power, Frieda, but I still
have the pain of sight. No. *(He covers the lovers up with a sheet.)* Every heart has a right to
at least one secret.

He takes out a white hanky, and wipes his face, as he moves to a chair downstage.

LAWRENCE.
Bring me my bow of burning gold ...
Bring me my arrows of desire ...
Bring me my spear of clouds unfurled
Bring me my chariot of fire ...
I will not cease from mental strife
nor shall my sword sleep in my hand
until ... *(Shakes his head, sits.)*

The WAITERS *take the lid off the large silver tray top in front of* CARESSE *to reveal a bust
of* LAWRENCE. CARESSE *begins work on it. The* OLD COUPLE *sit quietly upstage,
watching.*

Scene Three

Tête à Tête

The moulin de soleil.
Silence. LAWRENCE *slowly turns his head to look at* CARESSE.

CARESSE. Don't look at me! *(Pause.)* Find some patch on the wall and let it fire your
imagination. That way your eyes stay alive.

LAWRENCE *(staring forward)*. What wall? I see only Cagliostro's magic pool, with soft
white clouds slipping over it. And Frieda, standing, water lapping above her hip. A dark
shadow under the pool's skin, brushing the thigh. And lo! the young God surfaces, shaking
the wet from his hair. *(Pause.)* Give Harry a stick between his faultless teeth and he'd be the
perfect golden retriever.

CARESSE. So you can see through walls?

LAWRENCE. Can't you?

CARESSE. I've never cared to try. *(Looks away.)*

LAWRENCE. Will you leave my eyes blank, like the ancients? Endless images of Oedipus, and dead eyed gods.

CARESSE. That's how Harry sees you.

LAWRENCE. As long as he doesn't pester me with adoration.

CARESSE. It's not the adoration I fear, but the imitation.

LAWRENCE. But isn't that what your whole lives are based on? (*Pause.*) What do you see when you look at me?

CARESSE. If I could find the right words, I'd write poetry instead.

LAWRENCE. Not having the right words has never stopped anybody. More's the pity. Still, it's nice to know you think I'm worth a little verse. A limerick, perhaps. (*Extemporises.*)
There was a young lad from Eastwood
Who aimed to do all a beast could
He howled in a rage
When trapped in a cage
And spat out his soul in sweet blood.
(*Pause.*) I've been angry all my life. Now I'm angry and tired. It may well be a deadly combination.

CARESSE (*pauses*). I've never felt anger.

LAWRENCE. And yet you claim to love?

CARESSE. What has anger to do with love?

LAWRENCE. It's the buoy on the sea that marks the profound power.

CARESSE. I don't see it that way.

LAWRENCE. How do you see Harry's other women?

CARESSE. How do you know . . . ?

LAWRENCE. A little bird at Shakespeare and Co.

CARESSE. So you listen to gossip?

LAWRENCE (*smiles*). It's the divining rod into the dark self.

CARESSE. Harry has no dark self. Everything he does has to burn in the full light of the sun. Nothing is hidden. I sometimes wish it was. Sylvia Beach shouldn't talk of us. Still, what the great will do, the lesser will prattle of. But I had rather imagined you above all that.

LAWRENCE (*mildly*). I'm above nothing. As time passes, I simply slide further to one side. (*Pause.*) How do you feel towards these women?

CARESSE (*pause*). Harry loves me.(*Wrily.*) On our honeymoon, we sailed down the Nile together. It was there I discovered I was no Cleopatra. I lack the performing ability to be to him all women in one. Besides, marriage stripped me of the veil for him. When Harry sees a veil, he feels honour bound to pull it aside.

LAWRENCE. One veil or seven?

CARESSE. I no longer count the number. But I know one thing, whenever he does lift that veil, it is my face he finds there. He told me. It's me he sees at the moment of ecstasy.

LAWRENCE. How convenient for you. You save all that absurd expenditure of energy, and still retain possession. What a shit! At least when Frieda fucks her friends she has the decency not to imagine me. Put him on the pyre and burn the bogger!

CARESSE. You are cruel.

Silence.

LAWRENCE (*quietly*). Don't you imagine . . . I imagine her with
. . . It's like a fever. Sometimes I'm the gamekeeper again, sometimes I'm My Lady herself reaching into the dark, all too often now I'm the man in the wheelchair, trapped in the castle, sweating through a white night, as only my sight burns through the walls, forcing me to learn more of the lessons of love with no hope of bringing them into reality. (*Pause.*) I'd like to stop now.

CARESSE. Of course.

LAWRENCE (*moving across to her*). Too tranquil. Don't you get tired of self-portraits?

She tenses. He takes hold of her wrist, and rubs the chisel across his face.

LAWRENCE. Hack the skin off the stone. Don't bother if it bleeds. Only alabaster crucifixions have the perfect complexion.

LAWRENCE *returns to the bed, and pulls away the sheet.* ERIC *is revealed, alone, shivering. He begins to dress. The* WAITERS *clear the bed.*

ERIC (*sings*).
                    My Angeline
Endless nights of care, and watchful waiting
Do I wait in vain
Is it all in vain
Shall I be rewarded for my waiting
Will we meet again
Shall we love again?

My Angeline
When all is green in Arcady
you'll return to me, sweetheart
My Angeline
My every dream of Arcady
Makes me yearn for you, sweet heart.

The OLD COUPLE *remain, the* WOMAN *pulls a black shawl over her head.*

Two shrouded statues on either side of the stage.

The WAITERS *with lighted tapers begin to light candles below them. On the verandah the dim shadow of a shrouded crucifix.*

I know the road is always long
that leads to paradise
And just as long as we believe
in love or dying
My Angeline
When all is green
Then you'll remember
You wait for me in Arcady.

Scene Four

Les Deux Maries De Notre Dame

Incense. The chorus chant a latin mass. ERIC *stands waiting, uncertain. Behind him, a veiled woman turns with lighted candle. She slides it between his legs. He stares at it, horrified.*

ANGIE (*murmurs*). Master. Master.

He slams his hand down to extinguish it. He screams.

ANGIE. Angie. Kiss it best.

ANGIE'*s English is considerably improved, but all words that are the same in French, she pronounces in French, and those she cannot find she attempts to mime.*

ERIC. Better.

She kisses his hand. He takes her by the neck and kisses her.

ERIC. Oh, Christ. Come on, let's go home.

ANGIE. We must attend.

ERIC. For what?

ANGIE. Easter. (*Pause.*)

ANGIE. All the world attend. Angels. Saints. Santa Marie la Mere. Marie Magdalene, la fille de joie –

ERIC. The whore.

ANGIE. No, the girl of joy, she attend to embrace her amour.

ERIC. I know how she feels.

ANGIE. Patience. La Passion comes.

ERIC. Mine's a different passion from that of Magdalene and the Master.

ANGIE. But no. The same.

ERIC. Jesus didn't ... he was celibate. A monk. Le moine.

ANGIE (*laughs*). Men believe anything!

The OLD WOMAN *stares at them.* ANGELIQUE *whispers with her. The* OLD WOMAN *sighs, and lifts up her arms to the ceiling.*

ERIC. What did you say?

ANGIE. I say you are Anglais sinner.

ERIC. And desperate to sin again, my angel.

ANGIE. No.

ERIC. Don't got holy on me. Not tonight.

ANGIE (*mildly*). It is not a sin. (*She sits.*)

ERIC. What are you doing?

ANGIE. I confess.

ERIC. That should be worth money.

ANGIE. You want I confess to you?

ERIC. What could you confess to me that I don't already know? You think I want a coup à coup of how you spread your legs for some lecher in the Bois de Bologne? I can smell his parfum on you, tu pue le bouc, can smell his cheap cognac. You stink.

ANGIE (*unoffended*). Lick me to be cline.

ERIC (*touches her face*). Oui. Allons. S'il vous plait.

ANGIE. Attends. Attends le miracle.

ERIC. I don't believe in miracles. I'm English. We have bell ringing instead.

ANGIE. You must! The poor must believe!

ERIC. Perhaps I'm not poor enough.

ANGIE. Peut-être.

ERIC (*pauses*). I don't even know what a miracle is.

ANGIE. When some thing, some body, come again to life. (*Silence. Then*). If I confesse a miracle, you attend? Perhaps I give you une fable? Histoire?

ERIC. Story.

ANGIE. Then you confess to me?

ERIC. What?

She smiles, and pats the seat next to her.

ANGIE. Il était une fois . . .

He sits reluctantly between her and the OLD WOMAN.

ANGIE (*cheerfully*). Ma mère is called Mary. She die . . . en naissance –

ERIC. Giving birth.

ANGIE. The nonnes take me. Wash me, mais aussi they watch me, watch me all the time with eyes like . . . couteaux.

ERIC. Knives.

ANGIE. I turn my head, because . . . not good to look, (*Makes a slap.*) but wherever I look, all the time, all I see is the Master . . . sur la Croix. Head (*Tilts her head.*) eyes ferme . . . closed . . . he . . . fronce les sourcils?

ERIC. Frowns.

ANGIE. Like you frown now, but true. True pene. Pain. All the world, all the time, they watch him, but assistance, no. No (*Emphatically.*) help. I want to reach him. He cannot reach me, because . . . The hands. The blood with the . . . clous?

ERIC. Nails.

ANGIE (*nods*). I cannot reach him, he cannot reach me. He is the same as me. No assistance. Only Les Spectateurs de la Passion. (*Pause.*) Once, once upon a time, men put me in a cell, with the lock, with the . . . and men pay to be spectateurs. (*Mildly.*) Why?

ERIC. I don't know.

She relights the candle from her neighbour's, hands it to ERIC.

ANGIE (*smiles*). Saint Eric.(*Pause.*) Easter. Easter they cover my dead lover with the shroud. I, maybe twelve years, in a cell, in the convent. All the girls sleep, but for me une nuit blanche –

ERIC. A white night. Sleepless night.

ANGIE. But black. Dead candles. And in the black I see . . . white shadow, and he come to me, and puts his hand to my cunt, but he cannot touch me because there is not here the body, and then I see la ressurection is not . . . (*With difficulty.*) not inevitable, not . . . automatique. It is not a show to watch. It is for me to do. Assistance. I (*Smiling.*) make very soft feet off the bed. I enter the . . . chapel, I climb sur l'autel. The table. Under le chraoude, He is high. I cannot reach far, cannot pull away the . . . nails. But . . . I reach up. I touch him. Touch him. You understand? (*Silence.*) Et il tremble. (*In English.*) Tremble. In my hand. And I pull the chraoude, and I watch and his eyes . . . open. And I watch at my hand, and there is . . . le sang –

ERIC (*softly*). Blood.

ANGIE. – blood, like his, but no clou, clou, no nail, and the blood runs. He is . . . alive. And the blood drip drip on the cloth d'auteil between my legs. Then (*Shrugs.*) lights, arms, hands, they drag me lock me beat me, say the blood is my blood, say I am bad, and the blood . . . sec . . . comme d'or, like gold on my hand, and they wash me and beat me and try to make me cline. But I still bleed. And he . . . every year they kill him and send him to hell, where he attends his love. (*Simply.*) And every Easter I come to give him assistance from under the chraoudes.

Silence. She smiles and rises.

ANGIE. You watch. You see him move. (*Goes.*)

ERIC. What?

She darts upstage and disappears under the shroud.

ERIC. Angie! You can't . . . you can't be . . . Oh, my God! (*He bumps into the priest.*) Pardon. Pardon. (*Laughs nervously.*) Anglais pecheur! Mais je ne veux pas me faire confesser. Pardon. Nous sommes fous, n'est-ce pas?

The PRIEST *turns to the shroud. He ritually reveals the two side statues as the kneeling* MARY.

ERIC. I can't watch, don't you see. There's some things I don't want to see.

He goes.

The PRIEST *pulls the sheet down. A brilliant shaft of light blinds* ERIC, *and he turns away. The shadow of a crucified man cuts across the stage. The devotees put out the candles.*

THE SHADOW (LAWRENCE) (*reading*). Then the man who died said to his young cock, 'Thou at least has found thy kingdom, and the females to thy body. Thy aloneness can take on splendour, polished by the lure of thy hens.' And he left his bird there, and went on deeper into the phenomenal world, which is a vast complexity of entanglements and allurements. And he asks himself a last question: From what, and to what, could the infinite whirl be saved?

Silence. LAWRENCE *wears a rather shabby, single breasted, brown, woollen suit. Behind him a cloudy sky. He steps into the room.*

Scene Five

Le Coq Fugitif

The Moulin. Easter Sunday morning. The statuettes of the Marys have been replaced by two other covered shapes. And a gramophone. The OLD MAN *sits patiently watching. The* OLD WOMAN *tidies up from breakfast. As* LAWRENCE *continues reading from his manuscript.*

FRIEDA, *a robust middle-aged woman, in light dress and cardigan, finishes off a hearty breakfast.*

CARESSE, *in trousers, sips champagne. In front of her lie eggs she is painting.*

HARRY *in stripey sailor's top, paces the room, drinking and thinking.*

LAWRENCE (*reading*). So he went his way, and was alone. But the way of the world was past belief, as he saw the strange entanglement of passions and circumstance and compulsion everywhere, but always the dread insomnia of compulsion. It was fear, the ultimate fear of death, that made men mad. Men and women alike were mad with the egoistic fear of their own nothingness. And he thought of his own mission, how he had tried to lay the compulsion of love on all men. And the old nausea came back on him. For there was no contact without a subtle attempt to inflict a compulsion. And already he had been compelled even into death. The nausea of the old wound broke out afresh, and he looked again on the world with repulsion, dreading its mean contacts.

Silence.

HARRY (*quietly*). Yes.

LAWRENCE (*pleased*). Any more tea?

FRIEDA *pours him one.*

FRIEDA (*a deep voice with a trace of a German accent*). And you must have an egg, Lorenzo.

LAWRENCE. No.

FRIEDA (*firmly*). Yes. Caresse made them special.

She hands him a painted egg.

LAWRENCE (*amused*). Is my nose really that big?

HARRY. 'It was fear, the ultimate fear of death, that made men mad.' God, Lawrence, God, yes. but how do we break through that fear into the light of sanity?

LAWRENCE (*smiling*).
Humpty Dumpty sat on the wall
Humpty Dumpty had a great fall –

He drops the egg.

FRIEDA. Lorenzo is not a great admirer of other folk's art.

LAWRENCE. Because they daren't go beyond the breaking.

CARESSE (*smiling*). I don't expect my works of art to last for ever.

The WOMAN *stares confused at the egg. She goes to tidy it up.*

LAWRENCE. No (*Grandly.*)
All the King's Horses
And all the King's Men
Couldn't put Humpty Dumpty
Back together again.
As if politics and armies could ever be the great healer. Look at Germany.

FRIEDA. He loves to malign my Fatherland.

LAWRENCE. But isn't it true?

FRIEDA. I have not heard you yet, but of course it vill be. (*Hands him an egg.*) Here, take me.

LAWRENCE. Germany (*He drops the egg.*) Shattered by the war. And all the lunatic politicians do is try to glue the bits back together, with wild misreadings of Teutonic myths, to give them a cheap, quick feel of superiority. One day we'll have to pay for such folly. Just as we'll have to pay for the craziness of Bolshevism, and Americanism, twin ideologies of insanity. (*He takes up two more eggs.*) Both are based on grab, and greed. Of the two, Americanism is the worst. Bolshevism only takes your home, but Americanism smashes your very soul.

He tosses two more eggs in the air. HARRY *frowns, and takes up an egg. He drops it.*

FRIEDA. They so easily pick up bad habits.

HARRY. The one you missed. Englishism. The disease of stagnation and rotting eggs. On the whole, I consider it better to smash, than stagnate.

LAWRENCE. Why shop around for the best disease? They are all only differing facets of the same dead soul of the modern world. We artists must go beyond.

CARESSE (*to* WOMAN). Laisse les oeufs.

FRIEDA. Are there any hard boiled?

CARESSE. Here.

FRIEDA *proceeds to eat an egg.*

HARRY. How do we go beyond?

LAWRENCE. What is the next verse of Humpty Dumpty?

HARRY (*surprised*). I didn't know there was one.

LAWRENCE. Don't you feel there is one? But doesn't the voice of the child within us still cry out, 'What happens next?' And the artist betrays that child by daring to go no further, by leaving us always endlessly battered and bruised at the bottom of the hill, cracked at the foot of a wall, trapped down some dark hell of a slimey well. Instead of going on, he tries to divert us by playing formally with the broken pieces, reworking them into mere patterns of perversity.

HARRY. But how do we go on?

LAWRENCE. We travel on the ship of nausea.

CARESSE. Must the passage always be one of nausea?

LAWRENCE. A certain mal de mer of the soul is inevitable.

FRIEDA. It's a myth the English are great seafarers.

HARRY (*watching him*). Is there no port of call? Is there only isolation?

LAWRENCE. In the sequel I plan to The Escaped Cock, the man does come again to land. There he knows of nothing but his own fragmentation. He meets a priestess, a temple virgin dedicated to wait for the return of Osiris. She sees in his being, his battered body, his soul scattered to the far corners of the world, the image of her Lord waiting for her love to resurrect him. At first, so tentative to the pain of touch is he, so fearful of the compulsion of love, he denies this. But her attendant will guides him into a true life.

CARESSE. Her love heals him?

LAWRENCE. They ressurect each other, for she, too, has travelled through a similar vale of death, but in a different way.

CARESSE. What way?

LAWRENCE. Daily death by boredom, shame and swallowed rage.

CARESSE (*smiling*). And so they all live happily ever after?

FRIEDA. No.

CARESSE (*sincerely*). Isn't that how all true stories end?

FRIEDA *smiles.*

LAWRENCE. The tide of men again parts them, but not before there has been conception. The Child God. Not yet born, but waiting. That's as far as I can see.

Silence. LAWRENCE *pours another cup of tea.*

HARRY. He is born already.

LAWRENCE (*sharply*). What?

HARRY. The Sungod. He's born. I've seen him.

FRIEDA (*rising*). Shall we go for a walk? I'd love to pick some flowers.

LAWRENCE (*sharply*). What do you mean you've seen him? How can you have seen him?

HARRY. Yesterday morning, at dawn, as I flew through the clouds. Horus rose like a young boy from off the pillow, his golden head turned to whisper to me of the endless reality of poetry.

LAWRENCE. Flying through the clouds. Are you mad?

CARESSE. Harry has a plane, Lawrence.

HARRY. Come with me. I'll take you up to meet him.

FRIEDA. Lorenzo gets sick on boats, dear.

LAWRENCE. I don't get sick. I just hate the false throb of machines, giving you some safe imitation of sexual ecstasy.

HARRY. That may be true for you, but it's far from true for all of us.

LAWRENCE. What did you say?

CARESSE. Harry!

Silence.

VOICE. I cunt, ken you, ninny? I cunt, ken you, ninny?

FRIEDA *and* LAWRENCE *looks around.*

CARESSE *unveils the parrot.*

FRIEDA. What a wonderful bird.

She puts her hand on LAWRENCE.

CARESSE. And talented. He's the only parrot in the world that recites James Joyce.

LAWRENCE (*sullenly*). I should hope so.

CARESSE. He also lays eggs.

FRIEDA. He seems a little confused.

LAWRENCE. Wouldn't you be if you had to copy a madman who thinks you became a revolutionary simply by inverting the Christian cross? God save us from such inanity.

HARRY. That's cruel.

LAWRENCE. Only a fool thinks he can soften truth, without distorting it.

FRIEDA. A point Lorenzo and I have often disagreed upon.

HARRY. Are you then the only priest of the new faith?

LAWRENCE. Believe what you like.

FRIEDA. Pretty Polly. Pretty Polly.

CARESSE (*smiling*). That's my daughter's name.

HARRY. I just don't –

LAWRENCE. Go on with your endless parroting of the words gold and sun, as though the mere repetition of a mock litany will really usher in the New Dawn.

PARROT. Can you not do her numb?

LAWRENCE (*mocking*). Can you not do her numb?

FRIEDA (*to* CARESSE). What do you call –

HARRY. Are you the only one entitled to speak of death then?

LAWRENCE. What do you know of death? I face it in every breath.

CARESSE. Tiresias.

LAWRENCE. Your generation flirts with it, through the bars, as though you had it locked up with the rest of your private and perverse menagerie.

HARRY. I face the dark as much as any man.

FRIEDA. Walk, my love.

LAWRENCE. You play with your planes, and drugs and women, it's all a game – you'll meet death as lost as anyone. Your art is only gold painted egg shells. You are a hollow Easter, for all your talk of rebirth. The sun you say quickens in your blood is the faintest film of the real thing.

HARRY. At least the artists of my generation had the guts not to shirk the war.

CARESSE. Harry!

LAWRENCE. No, you ran to it, like lemmings dreaming on the thrill of life. More fool you in running to the killing.

HARRY. We didn't go to kill. We went to heal. I drove an ambulance.

CARESSE. Harry was almost blown apart at Verdun when –

LAWRENCE (*not listening to her*). Don't give me that. You came to play at cowboys on the open range.

HARRY. At least I didn't stand by, whining impotently.

PARROT. I cunt, ken you, ninny?

CARESSE. Shut up! (*Softly.*) Shut up, Tiresias!

CARESSE *covers up the cage. The men stand, facing each other, almost shaking with rage.* FRIEDA *puts on a record – Empty Bed Blues sung by Bessie Smith. The* OLD WOMAN *cleans up.*

FRIEDA (*joins in the song*).
I woke up this morning with an awful aching head,
I woke up this morning with an awful aching head . . .

(*Grins at* CARESSE.) I love this.

Bought me a coffee-grinder
Got the best I could find
Thought he could grind my coffee
(*Dances.*)
Cos he had a brand new grind.

She reaches out to LAWRENCE. *He just stares angrily at her.* CARESSE *half attempts to dance with* HARRY. *He shrugs her off. She turns back to the singing, dancing* FRIEDA.

They dance together.

He's got that sweet something,
I told my girlfriend Lou,
For the way she's drinking,
she must have gone and tried him, too . . .

LAWRENCE *takes off the record.* FRIEDA *defiantly continues to sing.*

FRIEDA.
When my bed is empty
makes me awful mean and blue
My dreams are getting interrupted
sleeping single like I do.

He smashes it over her head.

FRIEDA (*vehemently*). Shise Kairl! bist doo fair-rookt givorden! Macht zee dich veerklich zc vilt mit eera fairflixtn kafaymoola? Gile yar? Villst doo fikken? Pech leepsta! Hast arber nicht das tsoik dartsoo miner ich.

He walks out. Silence. The WOMAN *comes tentatively forward to pick up the pieces.*

FRIEDA. You speak German?

CARESSE *shakes her head.*

FRIEDA (*smiles*). Gut. I once smashed a plate on his head. In Cornwall. It was the war. (*Picking the pieces out of her hair.*) Lorenzo does not have a great love for the gramophone. He says he'd rather go to a seance. There you get the chance to answer the dead back.

CARESSE. He must be very trying to live with.

FRIEDA. He's my favourite child.

CARESSE. You get to see your children?

FRIEDA (*shrugs. Pause*). They are grown up now of course.

CARESSE. My daughter is sixteen.

FRIEDA. Does she visit?

CARESSE (*carefully*). Occasionally.

FRIEDA. We have such a lot in common.

She hands the remainder of the pieces to the old WOMAN.

FRIEDA (to HARRY). He knows you won't publish his *Lady*.

CARESSE. We might be interested in the Escaped Cock sequel.

FRIEDA. But that he has to write first. The other is finished. (*To* HARRY.) Like you, I see my Sungod, with his head on the pillow. Only I see him, not just at dawn, but also at the end of the day.

She leaves. HARRY *takes out his phial and swallows a pill.* CARESSE *watches him.*

HARRY. It's like having John the Baptist to stay.

CARESSE. I already have his head on a platter, m'lord.

She lifts the cloth off the bust.

HARRY (*studies it*). How deceptive the light can be. It's not real gold glinting his beard, but only the stain of clay. Pop him in the furnace. Cook the phoenix. Let's see if he survives the flame.

CARESSE. He doesn't claim to be a God, Harry.

HARRY. He certainly claims the Holy Ghost fires his tongue though, doesn't he? And what happens when that deserts him? Look at the filth he spouts then. Mud fantasies of himself as gamekeeper, mounting a quivering Frieda. Our Lady with the black hairs between her breasts. Imagine.

CARESSE. No.

HARRY. No. (*Pause.*) That's all he does – imagine, but no action. He is incapable of acting on his own vision.

CARESSE. The man is dying.

HARRY. He's terrified of it.

CARESSE (*carefully*). Aren't you?

HARRY. It's different for me.

CARESSE. Because you think you are dead already? (*Silence.*) It's not true. I've held you. I know the difference between a corpse and a living soul. (*Pause.*) Do you?

He moves away to a table.

CARESSE. Will you come for a walk?

HARRY. I want to write.

She leaves.

HARRY. Verdun. Seven four one, an ambulance. My buddies, bits of bodies flying through the air. I can feel slivers of them slice into me. Red Cross glinting in the sun, and the Bosch start to burn us with their big gun. (*Laughs.*) I'm not a hollow man, Mr Eliot. Those I love lament endlessly within me wanting to be free. (*Puts his head down. Eventually.*) How come I am left alive? Am I alive? I feel sick. God, mal de mer, even out here. In this desert. Boy, am I thirsty? Where's the oasis? Is there nobody to stretch their shadow over me? At the oasis maybe. Maybe there is a love that is not a mirage. (*Pause. Smiles.*) Lawrence, you're wrong. The drugs and drink and women don't help me hide. They take me back again. Let me see you, black angel. Don't cheat me. Meet me at the next oasis.

He remains seated, drinking, staring at his empty sheets. The OLD MAN *closes the shutters.*

Scene Six

La Belle De Nuit

The WAITERS *make up the single bed.* ERIC's *room. A hot summer's night.* ERIC, *sweating in vest and pants, sits at his table covered with his notes, a bottle, and an empty plate, on the opposite side of the dance floor. He drinks heavily.*

ERIC.
    Rose of Mandalay
    Though you're far away
    Every night I pray
    That we'll meet again one day.

Ask the stars above you
If I'm thinking of you
But you know I love you
My Rose of Mandalay.

Silence. Sound of lovemaking.

ERIC. Ta gueule! For God's sake, shut up! Allez-vous faire foutre!

He turns to see a tired ANGIE *standing in the doorway.*

ANGIE. You want I should fuck away?

ERIC. No. No. That's the last thing . . . (*Drinks.*)

ANGIE. Is there food?

He holds up the glass.

ANGIE. Let us eat, yes? And perhaps we do some dancing.

ERIC. I don't dance. Dance for me. I want to watch you.

ANGIE (*pause*). Let us go out, please.

ERIC (*pause*). I don't want to go out. I want to stay here for ever.

ANGIE (*pause*). Bad day?

ERIC (*laughs*). How was yours? Did you have a successful day at work, my dear?

ANGIE. You say we are not to talk of this.

She takes off her dress, and wipes herself down from a bowl.

ERIC (*obsessively wiping the sweat off his hands and face*). I want to talk about it. I'm really curious. I'm a writer. My imagination has to flow through every gutter. Were there one, many, how many times did you meet Jesus in the Bois de Boulogne? How many spirits did you raise tonight? And was it a kiss that stirred them, and was it the kiss of blessing on the blood red lips, or was it the kiss du diable in the darker shadows? Was it – (*Coughs heavily.*).

ANGIE (*holds out the flannel*). Wash. Cool down.

ERIC. I don't want to cool down. I like sweating. We sweat for very good reasons. Did you sweat for a good reason?

ANGIE. Why you do this?

ERIC. I need you to love me.

ANGIE. I love you.

ERIC. But how can I know? How can I tell when I don't possess the key sign of it?

ANGIE. What is this?

ERIC. Faithfulness.

ANGIE. Comment?

ERIC. Fidelity. Fidelité.

Silence. She stares at him.

ERIC. Money. Money. Money. If only I had the money, I'd buy all your time. Then I could be sure. Then the two of us could close the shutters and stay here, for eternity. Money. Look. (*Laying out the money on the plate.*) Look, this is it. Four hundred and fifty francs. It will hardly last us the summer. And nothing, nothing coming in. Lost the last of my pupils today. That slimey rat, Tardieu, turned up, asked if I sprechen die Deutsch, when I said no, he picked up his hat and went. Not so much as an au revoir. Money men know which way the wind is blowing. No one wants to learn English anymore. You're my last pupil, and you hardly make it a paying concern do you?

ANGIE. I can, I can, Eric. Not with the French, no, no the French in summer all go south, but now I speak American –

ERIC. I taught you English not American. You'll never understand them.

ANGIE. I can speak with them, of course, I can, but for them to speak with me, I must have clean clothes, clean lingerie, some parfum, then there can be real money. (*Urgently.*) Invest. Invest fidelité in me.

ERIC (*pause*). You want I should live off you?

ANGIE (*smiles*). All artists in Paris live like this.

ERIC. Not me. I don't want to sell you. I love you.

ANGIE. Is what I say not love too?

ERIC. I don't ask that sort of sacrifice. I'm no pimp.

ANGIE. A pimp is the man you love.

ERIC. No. No. I can't accept that.

ANGIE. Fou. Fou. (*Puts on her dress.*)

ERIC. What are you doing?

ANGIE. I must go out.

ERIC. Why?

ANGIE. You want we not eat to death?

ERIC (*blocking her way*). No, no, you're not to leave me. Please, stay. Just stay and talk to me. I'll not touch you. I'll give you a lesson for free. I must know some words of American. Subway. Sidewalk. Sugar. My little sugar.

ANGIE. Later.

ERIC. I can't teach you any more can I? I don't know the Yankees' particular brand of foul-mouthed obscenity. So does that end la leçon francaise, la leçon en l'art d'amour?

ANGIE. I come back.

ERIC. No, it has to change. You have to understand. It has to stop. You stay here, you stay here with me.

She moves to go past him. He grabs her and raises his arm to slap her.

ANGIE (*quietly*). You lock me up, and beat me again?

ERIC. Why do you say that? I've never hit you. I've never hit you.

She stares at him.

ERIC. How do you know . . . I've never told you about her, never told any . . . how can you . . . That was a long time ago. It's not like that for us.

ANGIE. You write me the story. Then they make the film. Then I play the girl. Then we both are riche.

ERIC (*shaking deliriously*). No. No. I'll never write that story. Just stay with me.

ANGIE. Of course.

He begins to laugh. It starts a coughing fit. She moves to the table to get his glass and holds it out to him. He turns away, still coughing. She looks at the money on the plate.

ANGIE (*sings*).
Que reste-t-il de nos amours?
Que reste-t-il de ces beaux jours?
Une photo, une photo de ma jeunesse.
Que reste-t-il de billet doux
Des Mois d'Avril, des rendezvous
un souvenir qui me pursuie sans cesse . . .

She picks up the money.

HARRY (*drunk*). Donnez un pourboire. Pour le pauvre garçon.

She takes the money and leaves. ERIC turns and stares at HARRY.

HARRY. Your little friend is leaving you to do the washing up.

ERIC (*pause*). There must be some misunderstanding.

He sees the money has gone. A WAITER stares angrily down at the plate.

HARRY. Of course. Nous sommes fous, n'est-ce pas?

ERIC. Angie!

He turns to see ANGIE standing in the doorway. A WAITER closes the door in front of her. ERIC moves forward. The WAITER blocks his way. The band begin to play.

HARRY. My black angel. Champagne! (*Takes out his phial.*)

BAILEY. That's the spirit, Eric. Cherchez la femme.

ERIC turns to find BAILEY sitting at his table.

BAILEY. Bon voyage, Eric.

Scene Seven

Le Mal De Mer

ERIC (*trembling*). What? Where are you going?

BAILEY. Not me. You.

ERIC. I don't want to go anyway. I'm too ill.

BAILEY. I warned you.

HARRY (*standing uncertainly*). I don't like it here.

The WAITERS swirl around in almost a dance of death, sweepng the sea-sick men around. The women (when they appear) are untouched by the sway of the 'boat'.

As parts of the closed shutters are open and closed by the WAITERS beyond the image of rain, and troubled seas.

ERIC. I have to eat, or I'm going to be sick.

ERIC tries to sit down to eat BAILEY's meal.

BAILEY (*sternly*). Pardon! You have to sing for your supper, my little poet.

ERIC (*beats it out to the tune of 'Que reste-t-il . . .'*)
Here lies the bones of poor John Flory
His story is the old, old story
Money, women, cards and gin
Were the four things that did him in.

O stranger, as you voyage here
And read this welcome, shed no tear,
But take what I give,
And learn from me how not to live.

BAILEY (*sighs*). Not really my cup of tea, old boy.

ERIC *turns towards* HARRY.

ERIC (*desperately*). I suppose it's hardly Baudelaire.

HARRY (*to* HEADWAITER). O mort, vieux capitaine, il est temps! Levons l'ancre! Au fond de l'inconnu pour trouver du nouveau.

ERIC. I'm going to be sick.

HARRY. Only a touch of mal de mer.

WAITERS (*sing*).
It's oceans of kisses
and oceans of love
And I'm on the crest of a wave.

Red lips that lure me
and blue eyes above
and I'm on the crest of a wave

Once it was low tide, low tide
I couldn't win
but now it's high tide, my tide
here I came rolling in

oceans of kisses
and oceans of love
and I'm on the crest of the wave.

They reveal a dying LAWRENCE, *in pyjamas, lying Pieta-like in the arms of* FRIEDA.

The WAITERS *take him.*

LAWRENCE.
Have you built your ship of death, O have you?
O build your ship of death, for you will need it.

He falls into the arms of a WAITER *who drags him around as if in a marathon dance competition.*

ERIC (*to* HARRY). Help me. I'm dying.

HARRY. Join the club.

CARESSE *appears by the side of* FRIEDA. *Another shutter opens to reveal* CARESSE, *in blue, by* FRIEDA, *in black.*

CARESSE.
I'm just a woman, a lonely woman
Waiting on the weary shore

I'm just a woman, that's only human
One you should be sorry for

FRIEDA.
Am I blue
Ain't these tears in my eyes
Telling you

CARESSE crosses to HARRY. BAILEY *leaps to his feet. She turns away from him.*

A WAITER *enters with a giant phoenix to* HARRY. ERIC *watches hungrily.*

HARRY.
Here the anthem doth commence:
Love and constancy is dead;
Phoenix and the turtle fled
In a mutual flame from thence.

CARESSE *reaches to* HARRY. *He turns away.*

BAILEY.
Boy, she likes to eat and how
I could buy her a steak right now
If only I could get a break
I'd buy her a cow
she's my suppressed desire.

ERIC *stares at him.*

HARRY. Co co rico. Co co rico.

HARRY *reaches into the bird's parson's nose, and pulls out a bouquet of red flowers. He turns to offer them to* LAWRENCE. *They droop.*

HARRY. I was never lucky with flowers.(*To* CARESSE.) Wave your magic hand over these.

She takes them. She passes her hand over them. They revive. She holds them out for HARRY *but he has moved away.*

CARESSE. I'm here, Harry. I'm always here. (*Sighs.*)

BAILEY *groans. The* WAITERS *immediately light a taper, as he takes out a cigar.*

LAWRENCE (*to* ERIC). And death is on the air like a smell of ashes! Ah! Can't you smell it?

ERIC. I can smell it.

CARESSE. Nausea.

HARRY. I'm burning. Burning.

He begins to pull of his sailor's shirt.

ERIC *turns back to* BAILEY, *fighting through the smoke. It starts a terrible heaving coughing fit in him.*

ERIC. There's other stories. I have other stories.

ERIC *turns to get his notes.* LAWRENCE *is there. He holds up the last sheet of the notes and eats it.* LAWRENCE *gently pulls the paper out of his mouth, instead it is a blood red handkerchief.*

The champagne cork explodes, LAWRENCE *falls softly back onto the white table, assisted by the* WAITERS. *They lay a cloth over him.* FRIEDA *sits by his side.* ERIC *clutches his chest. He puts his hand to his mouth, and draws out a red spotted handkerchief.*

HARRY *draws out a white handkerchief, and wipes his face.*

HARRY. Burning. Burning.

BAILEY. You're sick, Eric. Don't look to art for health. Garçon! The bill! Au revoir. (*He exits.*)

A WAITER *brings the bill.* ERIC *faints. Two* WAITERS *catch his arms. They dance him into the arms of two more, dressed in bloodstained white (as cooks). They pour the ice bucket over him.*

WAITER.
Rain.
It's so easy in the rain
there's no need to complain
if she's with you

to hold her hand and then
it's ten to one you'll kiss her
in the rain,
you'll kiss her in the rain.

ANGIE *appears through the shutters, and moves onto the dance floor. She wears white silk lingerie, a coronet and carries a Statue of Liberty torch.*

ANGIE (*sings*).
Gee but it's tough to be broke kid
It's not a joke it's a curse
My luck is changing
It's gotten from simply rotten
To something worse
Who knows one day I will win too
I'll begin to reach my prime
Now all I can see is what our end is
All I can sense is just my time

I can't give you anything but love, baby,
That's the only thing I've plenty of, baby
Dream a while, scheme a while
You're sure to find happiness
And I guess
All those things you've always pined for

She places the torch between his legs. ERIC *takes it and stares at it. She disappears.*

HARRY *takes off his shirt to reveal a tattoo on his back.*

HARRY. The sun burns me all the time but I can't see it.

CARESSE. I can.

FRIEDA (*as* CHEF *approaches with a cleaver*). I see my sun god with his head on the pillow. But I see him not only at dawn but at the end of the day.

HARRY. No. No. I don't need to see any more fractured corpses. I only want to see my black angel.

The CHEF *brings the cleaver down on the dead* LAWRENCE.

ERIC (*struggling*). I must get out of here. I must find her.

HARRY. Why, why is she hiding from me?

He takes a capsule, then stares at ANGIE. *As* ANGIE *dances, the* CHEF *takes* LAWRENCE'*s head on a silver tray on a trolley across to* FRIEDA.

FRIEDA (*sings*).
I'm told my destiny's a victim of love
When my heart commands I must obey
One hundred million lovers love to be loved
Each in their special way.

CARESSE.
My kinda love
Your kinda love
Keeps me believing
Although you're deceiving
My kind of love is one way to paradise.

FRIEDA *takes the lid off, to reveal* LAWRENCE'*s head.* ERIC *wanders around them, like an unseen ghost.*

FRIEDA (*to head*).
And my kind of lips
Your kind of lips
When love comes stealing
Encourage that feeling
My kind of love is one way to Paradise.

FRIEDA. Speak to me, my love. I can still hear you.

LAWRENCE.
I woke up this morning with an awful aching head
I woke up this morning with an awful aching head

She laughs.

LAWRENCE.
Altho' you're happy today
You may be gone tomorrow
Love comes just once
Don't be a dunce
When you need it
steal it beg or borrow.

They begin to move the trolley away.

FRIEDA (*following*).
I'm fond of you
You're fond of me
so tell me you love me
hug me and squeeze me
One way to paradise
(I mean there's no excursion).

She pulls a veil across her face, and exits.

An American, WALTER, *enters.*ERIC *turns to see* ANGIE *nearby.*

WALTER. Hi, Harry. Hi, Caresse. Fancy seeing you here. Been a long time.

CARESSE. Hi, Walter. How's the world of movies?

WALTER. Moving right on into talkies.

HARRY. Oh God! The ghost of Christmas past. What the hell are you doing here? I don't need an ambulance.

CARESSE (*to* WALTER). How long have you been in Paris?

WALTER. I've just shipped over.

CARESSE. You still mooning after Louise Brooks?

WALTER. She's filming in Germany.

ANGIE *dancing by* WALTER.

ANGIE. Louise? C'est moi. Je m'appelle Louise.

WALTER. Pardon?

ANGIE. Me. I am called Louise.

WALTER. You could be.

LOUISE. Or maybe she's just taken the part you offered her.

ERIC (*watching. Cries out*). No.

ANGIE *takes the torch back from* ERIC *and dances for* WALTER *as he sings.*

WALTER.
Every little beat that I feel in my heart,
Seems to repeat what I felt at the start,
Each little sign
Tells me that I adore you, Louise.

Just to see and hear you
Brings joy I never knew
But to be so near you,
Thrills me through and through.

She turns away from him, and playfully places the torch between WALTER'*s legs.*

ERIC (*cries out*). No.

ERIC *turns to see the* CHEF *with the chopper. He flees into the arms of the* WAITERS. *They stick his hands into a bowl of boiling hot water. He cries out.*

HARRY. I said she'd left you to do the washing up.

WAITERS *put a plate in each of his outstretched hands.*

ERIC.
Rose of gay Paree
Though you think you're free
Every night I pray
That we'll meet again one day.

Ask the man behind you
If I've really a mind to
But you'll know I'll find you.

SAM, *a chauffeur, enters through the shutters on the end of a lassoo followed by* TED, *a cowboy. He shoots his gun in the air. Everyone freezes. Silence.*

HARRY. And I looked and behold a pale horse; and his name that sat on him was death, and hell followed with him.

ERIC *stands terrified, arms outstretched, a plate in each hand. Everyone freezes.*

TED *fires two shots. The plates shatter. Silence. He fires again.* ERIC *slumps into the bowl.*

Music: Home on the Range.

Slow fade.

ACT TWO

Scene One
Le Virginian

The Moulin, December. 1929.
THe cowboy, TED KELLY, *now without guns, holding a golf club.*

WALTER *(onstage voice)*. Clytoris, Clytoris, wherefore art thou, Clytoris?

A shutter is opened to reveal CARESSE.

CARESSE. Sorry. I've tried but . . I don't think she wants to be a star. Leastways, not if she has to play a cow. I'm afraid Clytoris is only interested in her own pleasure.

WALTER *(laughing)*. OK, Ted, we'll cut the hogtieing. Action! Cue the Bad Guy!

TED *practises a golf stroke.*

CARESSE *(shouting)*. Harry! Mosey along!

HARRY *(voice)*. She won't mosey.

The OLD WOMAN *appears on the verandah holding a stick with a carrot on the end. They all turn and stare at her.*

CARESSE. Oh, my God! *(Runs to the verandah.)* Harry, Christ, Harry you can't ride Sybil up here!

The sound of HARRY *falling off.*

CARESSE. Jesus!

She disappears. TED *stares at the carrot, and then at* WALTER.

WALTER *(laughing)*. Harry's crazy.

ANGIE. He will really get his family to invest in the talkies?

WALTER. The Fairbanks's said he was well into it. He and Douglas spent the weekend swinging from the chandeliers.

ANGIE. Why not ask him straight on, instead of this charade?

WALTER. You don't understand how Harry works. Everything has to be a game, or he won't play. Sam, ready on the titles?

SAM *salutes him, and scrawls on some old cards.* HARRY *appears, helped by* CARESSE. *He packs two First World War pistols and the nearest of* CARESSE's *hats to a stetson.*

HARRY. The bastard bucked me!

WALTER. Could the lady with the carrot get out shot?

CARESSE *shoos her into the room, where she joins the* OLD MAN. HARRY *is well and truly drunk, not that the others are exactly sober.*

WALTER. OK. Harry, Ted's the good guy, wanting to start a new life as a homesteader. You want to run him off the range. Action!

HARRY. Howdee, pard'ner!

WALTER. It ain't a talkie, Harry.

HARRY. Why the hell not?

WALTER (*confidentially*). Don't upset the pro, please. He's particularly sensitive about talkies. Just mouth everything and we'll put the old title up, right?

HARRY *nods and mouths the line.* SAM *sticks up a makeshift card in front of* HARRY. *It reads* 'Howdee, Stranger.' CARESSE *holds* HARRY.

WALTER (*moving between* TED *and* HARRY). Right. We intercut a few close ups of heavy stares. No love lost. And then you hit him between the eyes with the next line, Harry.

HARRY. Fancy joining me in a black angel, pardner?

WALTER. Don't rewrite the script, Harry.

HARRY. You just said nobody's going to hear it.

WALTER. What about all those deaf folk who lipread?

HARRY (*pause*). Right. Right.

HARRY *mouths the line.* WALT *signals* SAM. *He holds up* 'We don't want no homesteaders round here.'

HARRY. Eh, this is fun.

WALTER. Close up shot of Ted. Frustration, fury. Reach for where your guns should be. Ye', now the rush of realisation, you remember that sacred oath you gave your wife on her deathbed, that you'd hang up your guns for life. Your gunslinging days are over!

CARESSE (*impressed*). That's wonderful.

TED *smiles for the first time.*

WALTER. Now the branding iron into the fire. Lift it up. We can almost hear the hiss. Close up of the iron. Smoke. (*He puffs cigar smoke all over it.*) Hold on the iron. We'll echo this shot later with the smouldering gun. See how the image captures his inner state, the poetry?

CARESSE. Divine.

WALTER. Harry?

HARRY. Fascinating.

WALTER (*excited*). Ain't seen nothing yet, brother. Then we move from that smoke of the smouldering iron into the swirling smoke of the saloon! The ivories tinkling. (*He calls to* CARESSE.) On in the mist of time into the Hades of the Crazy Horse Saloon!

HARRY. I could do with a drink.

WALTER (*to* TED). You don't have to like him, Ted. Frankly, the more you feel like murder, the better.

TED *looks as though he knows this.* WALT *signals* SAM. *He holds up* 'The Crazy Horse Saloon'.

Lights. The shutters are closed. The OLD COUPLE *sit quietly at a centre table, staring uncertainly at the whisky glasses in front of them.*

WALTER (*voice*). Bring on the dancing girls! Louise! Music. Something nice and appropriate.

CARESSE *picks out* 'Going to Meet my Sweety Now.' WALT *grins. He charges around puffing smoke, and slapping hats on the* OLD COUPLE *sitting at the table. Behind them, at either side, the covered bust of* LAWRENCE *(with cowboy hat) and the covered parrot cage.*

HARRY *stands watching.*

ANGIE, *(now renamed* LOUISE*) dances. Her costume aspires if only in its provocativeness, towards the spirit of the bar-room girl.*

WALTER. OK. Louise. Now you're singing in the bar, and you see this stranger (*indicates* TED.) You immediately feel there's something different about him. A pain. A sorrow. The look of a man who has died. This sorrow touches a chord in you. (TED *certainly looks pained.*) You sing and dance especially for him. OK? Sing, my angel.

ANGIE. But . . . er . . . I do not know this song.

WALTER. It's the heart of half the songs in the world. A young girl yearns to meet her lover. Pretend.

ANGIE. But you say the deaf . . . ?

WALTER. When they watch your lips they won't care if the words you sing are wrong. (*Kisses her.*)

CARESSE.
  Hey, hey, clear the way
  Looks like this is my lucky day
  I'm going to meet my sweetie now.

WALTER. Action!

ANGIE *mimes well to the song.* WALTER *moves around picking out the shots.*

CARESSE.
  Just can't be annoyed
  Am I happy I'm overjoyed
  I'm going to meet my sweetie now.

  Oh what kissing and oh what petting
  Oh what loving I'll soon be getting

WALTER. Louise, you're beautiful. I love you. Now you try and draw Ted into a dance. (*She attempts with a reluctant* TED, *desperately.*) Come on, Ted.

SAM (*decisively. In a Nottingham accent*). Cowboys don't dance.

WALTER. True. But look interested. Close up as we see he can't resist her.

ANGIE *runs her hand across his body.*

WALTER. Terrific. He's melting, honey.

Her hand slides down to his groin. TED *stares in amazement.*

CARESSE. You've got to hand it to her. She's subtle.

TED *sits quickly.*

ANGIE. This is wrong?

WALTER. Just sit on his knee, honey. Little does our hero realise whose gal he's taken in his arms. (*Moves to* ANGIE.) And now, my lost flower, who always puts her love in the wrong place, listen. The sound of hoofbeats. (*Grinning.*) You'd recognise those hoofs anyway.

ANGIE. Hoofs?

WALTER. You turn, trying to tear yourself away from our new lover's arms, but he holds on too tight. Too late. Wild Harry Hickcock is already à la porte.

HARRY *kicks over a chair.*

WALTER. We close up on the doors swinging behind him. Then wide shot. Run to him, honey. Spurn her. Spurn her.

He spurns her.

WALTER. The boy's good.

CARESSE. Great little spurner is our Harry.

WALTER. Cut to Louise, close up, biting back the tears.

ANGIE. Can I speak?

WALTER. No need.

ANGIE. Am I good?

> WALTER *kisses her.* TED *sighs.* SAM *hands him a drink.* HARRY *takes a quick swig from the bottle. The* OLD COUPLE *stare uncertainly at their glasses.*

HARRY. Bet you don't get the real thing on the set back home.

CARESSE. Not too much, Harry.

HARRY (*turning*). Ready when you are, boss.

WALTER (*reluctantly breaking away*). Louise, realising what Harry might do, rushes back to cover Ted. Harry stands, watching as his girl is all over the homesteader. He ain't exactly pleased. Imagine Caresse being mauled by some gigolo.

HARRY. What's new?

CARESSE. Once, Harry, once. And he wasn't a gigolo. He was a waiter.

HARRY. What's the difference?

CARESSE. What did you care?

> HARRY *shrugs.*

WALTER. Bad note. Forget it. Just look mean.

CARESSE. We were only dancing.

WALTER. Now drag her away.

> *A certain pulling to and fro, as* LOUISE *now rejects* HARRY, *amounting to a drunken gesture towards an Apache dance.* HARRY *throws* LOUISE *to one side.*

WALTER. A sudden silence. Back off, slowly. Harry realises our hero isn't packing.

ANGIE. Packing?

WALTER. He laughs. (HARRY *laughs.*) We see the humiliation Ted is experiencing, a humiliation intensified by being in front of a woman, the woman he loves.

CARESSE. Love at first sight, eh?

HARRY. It can happen.

ANGIE. Yes.

WALTER. Harry takes out one of his guns, and slides it down the counter.

> *The* OLD COUPLE, *oblivious, lift their glasses. The gun slides under them. They stare at it, not drinking.*

WALTER. Everyone back away now. The good guy stares at it. Take your time. (TED *throws him a look.*) OK. Great. Pick it up slowly. Tuck it in your belt. Now turn to him. Easy. Easy. Harry is still grinning.

CARESSE. Does the good guy ever get to smile?

WALTER. What's a good guy got to smile about? Maybe we'll let him have a little twitch in the last frame, before he gets to kiss the gal. (*To the* OLD COUPLE.) That may not be the best seat in the house, kids.

They are baffled.

CARESSE. Ces messieurs vont tirer des coups de pistolet dans un moment.

The OLD COUPLE *move away at speed, leaving the glasses behind them.*

WALTER. Easy does it. One last close up of your faces. A moment's uncertainty flickers across the eyes of the baddie.

HARRY (*grimaces*). How's that for a flicker?

WALTER. Hemingway couldn't do it better.

HARRY. That son of a bitch.

CARESSE. Harry can't forgive him for leaving him out of *The Sun Also Rises.*

HARRY. A title like that was made for me. 'Sides, I was there. It's me who ran the bulls not him.

WALTER. Yes, sure, so (*To* TED.) Back to our hero. Is he actually going to break his oath to his dying wife? How revolutionary is our movie going to be? Five . . . four . . . three . . . two . . . one . . . FIRE!

They draw. TED's gun fires. An unnatural high shriek. HARRY staggers as if shot, as he falls glasses smash around him. Silence.

TED (*furious. To* HARRY). Shise kairl! Bist doo fair-rookt givordn? (*To* WALT.) This is all vrong! You said he vas to vound me.

WALTER (*confused*). OK, so slight change of plan, so let the kid have his way, Ted. What the hell . . . We're pros, aren't we? We can bail ourselves out.

Silence.

TED. It's not right. It is vrong.

WALTER. Just give me a break. Let me think . . .

CARESSE. Let's just bury him in Boot Hill.

ANGIE. I nurse him.

WALTER (*desperate*). Brilliant! We see her, tears in her eyes. The girl truly loves him even though he's a –

CARESSE. Merde.

ANGIE. I understand.

WALTER. Go to your love. A last shot of the good guy, baffled, confused, the gun still smoking in his hand. Then we cut to the girl cradling the bad guy in her arms.

She cradles HARRY *in her lap.*

CARESSE. You want some appropriate music?

WALTER. Anything.

CARESSE *hammers out the* Funeral March.

WALTER (*looks at her. Sighs*). OK. And then, the final shot, as she looks up, tears in her eyes, but with the faintest smile of hope like a rainbow breaking through the rain. (*Pause.*) Cut. End of movie.

CARESSE *applauds. The* SERVANTS *join in.*

CARESSE. God, how I love a happy ending.

WALTER. And that, mes amis, is how we make a silent movie. And now we normally have a party.

CARESSE. Champagne!

TED *takes* WALTER *on one side.*

TED. I played your game. You keep your word.

WALTER. Cross my heart. I'll dub 'Dust on the Plain' without a soul being any the wiser.

SAM. It's an art, you know. It's Ted's art you're playing with.

WALTER. I'm not playin'.

ANGIE *screams.*

WALTER. We've finished, my love. Le film est fini.

ANGIE *holds up a bloodstained hand.*

WALTER. Oh, Jesus, no.

CARESSE. Harry!

HARRY'*s body rolls over. Oblivious, the* OLD MAN *pops the champagne.*

SAM. The gun!

WALTER. Didn't you check the fucking thing?

TED. Harry. They are Harry's. He give me.

WALTER. Oh, God.

CARESSE (*crossing over*). Come on, Harry. Stop playing for God's sake. Harry! Please.

Silence. She holds him.

CARESSE. Speak to me. Please.

HARRY (*eventually*). How can I speak to you? I'm dead.

Silence.

SAM. The bloke's barmy.

CARESSE. Oh, Harry, Harry! (*She gets up and walks away.*)

HARRY. Is there no respect for the dead anymore?

ANGIE. Is he all right?

WALTER (*forces a laugh*). You old trickster. Should have known better. Even during the war, Harry Crosby still played his practical jokes.

CARESSE. He was a kid then. High time he grew up. High time you all grew up.

TED. We vish to go. I am an actor. I am sane. I do not wish to be among mad folk.

WALTER (*confidentially*). Nearly there, nearly there. Please.

ANGIE. The blood on my hand.

HARRY (*holding up his hand*). Me, too.

WALTER. He must have cut it on the glass.

ANGIE. You have . . . les echardes.

WALTER. Splinters.

HARRY. Help me.

ANGIE. Let me see.

 She takes his hand. WALTER *sighs.*

SAM. Splinters can be a right bogger. Remember when you roped me to that tree?

TED (*smiling*). But I also cut you free.

SAM (*grins*). What did you call me?

TED. My lonely cactus.

CARESSE. What's that?

TED. A private joke about a private tree.

CARESSE. Oh, sorry.

ANGIE (*to the* WOMAN). Un bol d'eau chaude. Vite!

 The OLD WOMAN *goes out.* WALTER *attempts to keep the party spirit going.*

WALTER. Should have known better than to panic. Harry's always been lucky. Anyone who can walk away from seven four one can survive anything.

ANGIE. Seven four one?

WALTER. The ambulance Harry drove at Verdun.

ANGIE. Perhaps my father was there.

HARRY. Perhaps Ted Kelly was there. (*Pause.*) Is that a German name?

CARESSE. Harry!

WALTER. We were driving across No Man's Land –

HARRY.
Red cross glinting in the sun
and the Bosch start to burn us with their big gun –

SAM. Don't call the Germans Bosch.

HARRY. Mere alliteration. No offence.

TED. Not offended. I am not German now, I am American. (*Pause.*) But maybe now I have to become German again.

 SAM *holds his hand.*

ANGIE. What happens?

CARESSE. Let it go.

ANGIE. I will like to know.

WALTER. Harry's driving, I'm in the back, when all hell breaks loose. I'm tossed clear over the tailgate, then seven four one takes it right on the nose. The whole thing just shattered into a thousand pieces. (*Pause.*) Bits of bodies flying unaided through the air. I thought bye bye Harry. And then out of the smoke, I hear this voice.

ANGIE. What does it say?

WALTER. 'Let's go get a drink.'

HARRY. I was so thirsty.

WALTER. And I look up and lo and behold there shining in the light is lover boy. Not a scratch on him. I just couldn't credit it.

HARRY. You were right not to. I was dead. Only I've just remembered. I am the ghost of Christmas Past.

CARESSE. Enough, Harry.

ANGIE. You are charm . . . er . . .

HARRY. Charming?

ANGIE. No.

HARRY. Oh, dear.

ANGIE. Charmed!

HARRY. I'm charmed to meet you. Who is this lady?

WALTER. Louise.

HARRY. Louise, we have met before.

ANGIE. No.

HARRY. Must have been some other life.

WALTER. You OK, old buddy?

HARRY. Hunky dory.

WALTER. Maybe we could have a little chat sometime.

HARRY. Sure thing, pardner. (*To* ANGIE.) You're very gentle.

   The OLD WOMAN *arrives with the hot water, and towels.*

HARRY. What's that for?

ANGIE. We wash the hand.

HARRY. No. (*Rising.*) To the magic pool. The magic pool will cure me.

ANGIE. Magic pool?

CARESSE. You'll freeze to death.

HARRY. The waters of life, Caresse. Come on, a last skin dip in the dying embers of the sun. Who knows when we'll see it again. It's going to be a long dark winter. Come on, Walter.

WALTER. I never was one for sport, Harry.

HARRY. Sport? Only a communist could confuse spiritual ablution with exercise. What about you two? Come on, Sam. You're an old sailor, are't you?

TED. Because he vas a sailor, dos not mean he can svim.

HARRY. Caresse, come with me. (*Pause.*) You used to.

CARESSE. I've got something painful on my chest right now, Harry.

HARRY (*pauses: then to* ANGIE). You're my last hope.

She smiles. WALTER *frowns at her.*

CARESSE. Scared of going on your own Harry?

ANGIE. I'd like to see it.

HARRY. Good girl.

WALTER. Don't strip off, honey. (*Pause.*) You'll catch a cold.

ANGIE (*ambiguously*). I won't.

She smiles and follows HARRY *out.*

TED. We need to get back to the hotel.

WALTER. Give me ten, please.

TED *sighs.* SAM *smiles at him.* SAM *looks through the records by the gramophone.*

SAM. Got ought to dance to?

CARESSE. Were you really a sailor?

SAM. Stoker.

WALTER. Ted stowed away on his boat in Hamburg in '19.

CARESSE. And now you're going back to Germany? Isn't it a bad time for a Jew there?

TED. Where is it good?

WALTER. Tougher for the communist.

SAM (*smiles*). That was a long time ago.

WALTER. There's still something to it.

SAM. I dunno.

TED. Give us love any day.

WALTER. I kinda thought that was what it was.

SAM *selects a record. He puts on orchestral version of* Crest Of A Wave, *and begins to sing softly.*

Do I seem to effervesce
My baby says maybe
And maybe means yes
He's a dream to gaze upon
He's lovely he's gorgeous
And from now on

TED *smiling moves across to him.*

It's oceans of kisses
And oceans of love
And I'm on the crest of a wave

TED *joins in with him. They hold hands, and slowly begin to sway to the music.* CARESSE *watches them, almost enviously.* WALTER *sits by her.*

CARESSE. Doesn't Ted ever take his costume off?

WALTER. It isn't a costume.

CARESSE. Poor old Sam. Forced to masquerade as a chauffeur wherever they go.

WALTER. I guess he considers it a small price. Love is sacrifice.

CARESSE *bursts into laughter, then stops suddenly.*

WALTER. You OK?

She looks at him, then pours a double.

WALTER. And Harry?

CARESSE. High in the clouds. But he's flying solo nowadays.

She stares down at the broken glass.

WALTER. Is that by choice?

CARESSE (*pause*). Can't find a forwarding address. It's all over. It was wild while the gang were here, but now Bob McMahon, Hem, even Ezra, all blown away on the wind. Only Harry doesn't know where he's flying to. So he just heads straight out into the sun. (*Pause.*) He's burning out. Once I warmed my soul on that. Now I can't bear to watch it.

WALTER. I'll talk to him. I have to, anyway. (*Pause.*) You think I ought to check he hasn't drowned?

CARESSE. Louise is there.

WALTER. I hope she doesn't go for a swim. (*Pause.*) She's very fragile.

CARESSE. Is Louise her real name?

WALTER (*pause*). Sure.

CARESSE. How apt. Harry calls all his lovers names like the Woman of the White Horse, the Shadow, the Sorceress.

WALTER. How do you know?

CARESSE. I read his diary.

WALTER. That's not nice.

CARESSE. I know. But he insists. (*Pause.*) I wonder what name he will give to little Louise.

WALTER. I'm going to get them.

CARESSE. No need. They're on their way back.

WALTER. Developed second sight, have you?

CARESSE. It gives me no pleasure.

HARRY *and* ANGIE *return. He is shivering, in his pants.* ANGIE *is in her slip, carrying her dress and towel.*TED *stops suddenly, and takes the record off.*

HARRY. Cognac! (ANGIE *starts to dry him.*) Merci, ma vierge vestale.

WATLER *glances towards* CARESSE.

CARESSE. Harry has a remarkable imagination.

The OLD MAN *hands him the drink.*

HARRY. Oh, God, that's better! Slowly, slowly the life is beginning to flow in me. This girl of yours is an angel, do you know that?

WALTER. Yes. Aren't you cold, my love?

ANGIE. I warm myself on Harry's sun.

CARESSE. I bet.

WALTER. Sorry?

ANGIE. Look!

HARRY *turns*, ANGIE *takes the towel away to reveal his sun tattoo.*

ANGIE. Voila!

Silence.

WALTER (*attempting a joke*). One hell of a case of sunburn, Harry.

SAM. Makes my little anchor look a bit feeble.

TED (*smiling*). I tell you, size is not everything.

WALTER. Where did you get this?

ANGIE. On a boat, on the Nile. He sat on a red mat, in meditation.

HARRY. Done by a Hindhu sun sect who all have the tattoo on their bodies.

TED. How romantic.

CARESSE. Sure. While they held onto Harry's arms, the other sailors took the opportunity to grope me. All Harry could do was watch. At the end of this spiritual experience, Harry paid them in gold. Did you tip them, Harry? I can't remember. Did you?

Silence. HARRY *stands, and puts on a white shirt.*

CARESSE. The tattoo bled through his shirt, forming a perfect copy. Harry keeps it for his shroud.

She pours herself another drink. HARRY *stares at her. She looks at him.*

CARESSE. Change your shorts, Harry.

HARRY (*carefully*). They are not wet, mummy.

She looks at WALTER. *He reaches to touch* ANGIE's *hair.*

ANGIE. It will dry.

Silence. SAM *rises.*

SAM. I'll get the car.

WALTER. Right, ye'. Ye', we'd best be off. (*To* HARRY.) I said I'd take them to La Revue Negre.

ANGIE. Walter says Josephine Baker is dancing bananas.

WALTER. Nearly. Put your dress on, sweetie. (*Pause.*) Listen, why don't you guys come along? Start the Christmas parties with a bang, eh?

HARRY. Great. I've got to come up anyway to pick up the new Lawrence.

CARESSE. Not tonight, Harry. Tonight Polly is arriving.

HARRY. What?

CARESSE. Tonight I am seeing my daughter.

WALTER. Ah.

HARRY. We might join you later.

WALTER. Louise and I could hang on and catch a lift with you
if –

CARESSE. We couldn't guarantee if Polly would want to do that, could we, Harry? Not after such a long journey.

Silence. HARRY *mouths something at* WALTER, *and continues to dress.*

WALTER. OK, everybody. Saloon time.

TED (*formally*). Thank you all very much. It has been an experience.

CARESSE. Good luck in Berlin.

TED. Thank you. Goodbye, Harry.

HARRY. Guten targ.

SAM. Have a Merry Christmas.

CARESSE. And you.

TEd *and* SAM *leave.*

WALTER (*to* CARESSE). If I don't see you tonight, er . . .

ANGIE (*smiling*). Perhaps in New York.

HARRY. New York?

ANGIE. Walter take me to New York to be in the films.

HARRY. Do they make films in New York?

ANGIE (*laughing*). Of course.

CARESSE. Yes, yes, maybe in New York.

HARRY. What?

CARESSE. Everybody seems to be going home, I want to go home.

HARRY. This is home.

CARESSE. We could make it for Christmas, Harry. Come with me, Harry. WIll you come with me? I'm supposed to go everywhere with you, come with me. Let's sail back together, just you and me. You won't, will you?

She turns away. HARRY *and* WALTER *exchange glances.*

WALTER. Let's go.

CARESSE. Goodbye.

HARRY. Au'voir.

ANGIE. Au'voir.

WALTER *and* ANGIE *exit.*
Silence. She pours herself a drink.

HARRY. What's all this nonsense about Polly arriving?

CARESSE. You are quite right, Harry. It is nonsense. She is in New York. Where else would she be? I just imagined her coming here. We all imagine what we want, then realise what nonsense it is. I just imagined spending Christmas with someone I love, and who loves me.

HARRY. And don't I love you?

CARESSE. Don't make it a question, Harry. Make it a strong bold statement.

Silence.

CARESSE (*drinks*). What do you see in her? Don't tell me that it's me. I don't believe that any more. Why do you want to hurt me?

HARRY. I don't. (*Pauses. Quietly.*) It's just you don't inspire me any more.

CARESSE. Is that all I was for? (*Quietly.*) It seems . . . inadequate, Harry. and it makes me . . . angry.

She takes the sheet off the bust of LAWRENCE.

CARESSE (*pause. Laughs*). Oh, Lorenzo, you did tell me. I can hear you still. Taisez-vous. Taisez-vous.

She puts her hand over his lips.

HARRY. He haunts you as well. Why don't you kiss him, Pygmalion, and maybe he'll come alive?

CARESSE. I'm not like you, Harry. I don't sleep with my creations. I see that as a breach of professional ethics.

HARRY. He's possessed you.

CARESSE. It's childish to be jealous, Harry. All that's left of Lawrence is a voice.

HARRY (*distressed*). That's the one thing I don't have. I can't live with that. All I know is that if I could get to the sun, I could sing, I know I could.

CARESSE. So Harry Crosby gropes forward in the dark, onto the unknown girl, up into the unknown cloud, over the unknown wave hoping to come to the new found land.

HARRY. Is that so funny.

CARESSE (*pauses*). It is a comedy of sorts, Harry.

HARRY. I'm scared to go alone. Come with me.

CARESSE (*after a long pause*). I've no more space for your excursions. Every wave slaps me in the face. Constant nausea. It seems now strangely . . . unnecessary. Go to her. Don't come back Harry. Know tomorrow there's no Caresse upon the pillow. Give me a break, Harry. I'm tired of looking out to sea. This time be Columbus, not the Staten Island Ferry. (*Pause.*) Bon voyage.

HARRY, *now dressed in black evening suit, turns to go. He stops for a moment and looks back. The* OLD MAN *slowly closes the shutters on him.* CARESSE *nods for the* OLD WOMAN *to tidy up the broken glass. As she does so,* CARESSE *sings* 'Am I blue?'

CARESSE. I'm just a woman, a lonely woman
Waiting on the weary shore
I'm just a woman, that's only human
One you should be sorry for

Woke up this morning alone about dawn
Without warning he was gone
How could he do it
Why should he do it
He'd never done it before
Am I blue
Ain't these tears in my eyes
Telling you

Am I blue
Why you'd be too
If each plan
With your man
Does fell through

There was a time
When I was the only one
But now I'm the sad and lonely one
lordy

Was I gay
Until today
Now he's gone and we're thru'
Am I blue.

Why do you ask me if I'm blue
Ain't these tears in my eyes
Telling you.

The OLD WOMAN *holds up the cloth from the bird cage. The cloth is torn. Inside, the parrot lies dead. The music continues softly under the speech.*

CARESSE (*softly*). I know. The innocent always get caught in the crossfire. (*Wrily.*) We should never have named you Tiresias – it hardly augured well. (*Pause.*) No one can tell another the difference between art and reality, but we all pay the price for it. I can't tell who these tears are for. Does this make you happy, Lawrence? I'm angry, now what do I do? (*Pause.*) Silence. You're quite right. It's folly to ask an artist for advice. (*Turning to the* OLD WOMAN.) Burn it, Margueritta, burn, and then pack. Brules et emballes. Burn and pack.

Scene Two

Sous les Toits de Paris

The kitchen. Sudden chaos. Shadowy figures of fast-moving waiters.

A low working light over a sink. The CHEF *holds* ERIC's *head down into it, then lifts him out, coughing, spluttering, fighting for breath. he is almost weeping with rage and exhaustion, as he washes up. The* PLONGEUR *looks at him, curious.*

ERIC. Are these real tears? (*Desperately.*) How can you tell? Perhaps it's just my eyes sweating. We sweat for a very good reason. If only I knew what it was. There isn't a reason for this hell except that a few demand heaven. I see that clearly now. Much good it does me. (*The* PLONGEUR *smiles.*) I feel I can confess to you, because you can't understand. That's some solace. If you laugh at me, you don't really harm my vanity. I demanded heaven, too. Do you dream of heaven, I used to dream, I dreamt of being a writer.(*laughs.*) How sad. Look at me, my hands are so boiled in burning pans, I can hardly hold a knife, let alone a pen. Not that I've anything to write anyway. Oh, I know, you say why not write about this, but you can't tell, you can't sell, the truth, can you? Folk won't buy work that puts them off their dinner. Even if you tell them how they're being poisoned, they won't thank you, they'd rather cut out their eyes, than see. More fool them. Why should I care? I've been poisoned too. I loved, you see. Love destroys more than leprosy. Sheer folly. Fou. Fou. Eric. (*To* PLONGEUR.) Not you. Me. Oh, Angie, just because I said I didn't believe in miracles didn't mean I didn't want to. I want to see you. I need to see you.

The PLONGEUR *stops him, and gently wipes his eyes with a filthy teatowel.* WAITERS *put shirt and coat on* ERIC.

Music: (not sung) 'I'm Going to Meet My Sweetie Now'.

A red sheet is laid over the bed. By it ANGIE *stands, swaying to the music, silently miming the song. She slowly slips off her dress.*

ERIC. I'm so tired. (*Pause.*) So tired. I could kill for a moment's energy. (*Exhausted.*)
Eh ho, what a day
Looks like this is my lucky day
I'm going to meet my sweetheart now.

ANGIE *smiles, and reaches out slowly. All the* WAITERS *take off jackets, etc and sit, or lie, exhausted around the acting area at the end of their shift.*

The CHEF *places a tray in* ERIC's *hand.*

One WAITER (WALTER) *back to audience stands up stage, jacket over his shoulder. Light change.*

ANGIE *sings the remainder of the verse from* 'I'm Going to Meet My Sweetie Now'. *She turns upstage to sing the chorus to* WALTER. ERIC *exits.*

Oh, what kissing and oh what petting
And oh, what loving I'll soon be getting.

Scene Three

L'Hotel des Artistes

A hotel bedroom.

WALTER (*groaning*). How can a man think of love with money on his mind?

Silence.

ANGIE. You are not rich? (*Long pause.*) But all this . . . ?

WALTER. Une façade. Bait. With me at the end of the hook, and if Harry doesn't bail me out . . . (*Pause.*) God, when I was a Communist I never dreamt I'd end up playing Russian Roulette with Harry Crosby as my gun.

ANGIE (*pauses*). Don't worry. He will come.

WALTER. It's too late now.

ANGIE. Then tomorrow. He will come tomorrow. It will come good, believe me.

WALTER. It needs a miracle. (*He shivers.*)

ANGIE (*smiles*). You are cold?

She places his hand on her, then slowly slips her hand down his body.

ANGIE. Come to bed.

Slowly pulling him on top of her, she murmurs her soft litany of obscenities. Groaning, WALTER *pulls the sheet over them.*

HARRY *stands by the side of the bed, watching them. He carries the flowers.*

HARRY. It's one hell of a talkie, Walter.

WALTER *surfaces.*

HARRY (*slightly slurred*). Sorry, is this a private showing?

WALTER. Jesus, Harry.

HARRY. I understand. Two's a tête-à-tête, three's a ménage-à- trois. Just say the word, master, and I go. I go. (*Clicks his fingers.*) Gone.

ANGIE. Stay. Please. We want you.

HARRY (pause, grins). Good show.

WALTER. What?

HARRY. Baker, and the bananas.

ANGIE. Divine.

HARRY (*amused*). Divine?

ANGIE. She's black, black American. But she lives now in France.

HARRY. Sure. Blacks are like poets – America is only too keen to export them if they sing too loud. You didn't bring any bananas back with you, did you? I'm starving.

WALTER. We were expecting you there.

HARRY. Ye', well, I had to see an oriental sage about a . . . spiritual . . . and of course . . . I had to get these for my lady of the flowers here. You are beautiful, mam'selle. (*Hands them to her.*) I'd give them a drink if I were you, before they wilt away. You could do the same with me. Where's the bottle?

He takes the cloth off to find an empty bottle.

WALTER. Must have just run out.

HARRY. It's not New York, Walter. You can't run out of booze in Paris. They built the city for drunks and lovers. (*Sits on the edge of the bed by the phone.*) What's the room number?

WALTER. 750.

HARRY. Not 741? (*In telephone.*) Bon soir, champagne! And a bowl of fruit for the lady. With bananas. Sept cent cinquante. Merci.

WALTER. Go put them in water, honey.

ANGIE. Why?

WALTER. And put some . . . Please, OK.

She smiles at HARRY and exits.

HARRY. Lucky boy.

WALTER. Caresse not with you?

HARRY *rises and opens the shutter to reveal a full moon and a starry night.*

HARRY. Paris. The ideal setting for romance. How you figure your love will translate to the world of sky scrapers?

WALTER. It'll survive anywhere.

HARRY. I meant her. How will she translate? You really going to make her a star?

WALTER. Sure.

HARRY. Don't lie to her, Walter. It's not nice.

WALTER. She would live in a garret if need be.

HARRY. But could you?

WALTER. Done it before. (*Pause.*) Harry, I've been wanting to talk to you about . . . talkies.

HARRY. So talk.

WALTER *perches nervously.*

WALTER. They're opening up a whole new world right now, Harry. In a time of depression, folk will stand round the block for an image of another world. We're sitting on a gold mine here.

HARRY. Is this the voice of the man who used to chant the Communist manifesto as we carted corpses?

WALTER. I'm not talking money, Harry, well not .. . I'm talking vision here. The movies have grown up. They've learnt to speak. Now what they say, Harry, what they say, well, that could be the new poetry.

HARRY. Howdee, stranger.

WALTER. Doesn't have to be. Not if writers like Harry Crosby are right at the heart of it.

HARRY. What are we talking here, cowboy pictures?

WALTER. One example.

HARRY (*groans*). Jesus.

WALTER. You ever seen a cowboy film?

Behind WALTER, ERIC *enters with a tray with champagne, and a bowl of fruit.*

HARRY (*seeing him*). Stick 'em up, pard'ner!

ERIC *drops the bowl, and ducks down behind the trolley. Beyond him,* ANGIE *enters, holding a vase. She sees the gun on her, and drops it.*

WALTER. For God's sake, Harry!

ANGIE *kneels down to pick up the flowers. For a moment, it looks as though she and* ERIC *might meet as he crawls around picking up the fruit.*

WALTER *steps over him.*

HARRY (*rising*). Pardon! Pardon! I was never lucky with flowers.

WALTER. You OK, honey! (*He kneels by her.*) Harry and I were just working an idea for a movie. (*He kisses her.*)

HARRY *pops the champagne cork.* ERIC *cries out, and jumps up as if shot.*

WALTER (*to* WAITER). Allez! Allez! Fous-moi le camp!

ERIC *backs out, quickly.*

ANGIE. You should not speak with him like that.

WALTER. I'm sorry, honey.

ANGIE (*rises*). You must give him a tip. (*Sees he has already gone.*)

HARRY. Next time.

WALTER *crawls around clearing up.*

ANGIE. So you are playing a film?

HARRY. Sure. Cowboys and Indians. Walter and I are Americans, we're fascinated by frontier country.

HARRY *takes out his pills.*

ANGIE. What is that?

HARRY (*to* ANGIE). You care to try?

WALTER. No.

HARRY. If you're really going to the States, you'd better be open to new experiences. Try one, ma vierge vestale.

WALTER. Will you stop calling her that?

HARRY (*pauses*). I doubt it. (*To* ANGIE.) Come on. This'll fly you across the Alantic quicker than the Spirit of St Louis, Louise. Trust me.

She takes it with some champagne. HARRY *sits by her, as she lies on the bed.*

WALTER. Harry? About the –

HARRY. The problem is, Walter, I'm not sure that cowboy stories interest me. This (*Takes out a small book from his pocket.*) Now this is the only story right now that gets me going.

ANGIE. What is that?

HARRY. Smell. Smell. Fresh from a hot press. Uncut. Virgin. Vierge. A tale to change the world. Let's slice it open, so we can hear it speak.

He cuts the book with the fruit knife.

ANGIE. What is it about?

HARRY. It's about a man who has been crucified, but who, after three days, rolls back the rock of his burial place and walks dead through the world, trying to find a love pure enough to bring him back to life again.

ANGIE. Jesus?

HARRY. The man has no name now.

ANGIE. I know it is Jesus.

HARRY. You recognise him already? No one else did.

ANGIE. I have seen him many times.

WALTER (*dejected*). Biblical stuff is out now we've got talkies. Who's going to buy the Messiah speaking with a Bronx accent? (*Pause.*) Maybe we could make it as a cowboy, Harry.

HARRY. What?

WALTER. Harry. Maybe the honest cowboy is the modern Christ. Look, there's so many parallels in the story. The struggle for good over evil, the lone man, the mythic landscape.

HARRY. Mary Magdalen in the Crazy Horse.

WALTER. Isn't it her? Isn't it?

ANGIE. And the crucifixion?

WALTER. The good guy's always torn apart, and then is tended back to life by the love of a fallen woman.

HARRY. The priestess of Isis.

ANGIE (*urgently*). That's my part. I can bring Hickcock back to life. I can. I can.

Silence. HARRY *stares at her.*

WALTER. You're wet, honey.

ANGIE. What?

WALTER. You've water from the vase all over you. Don't want to catch a chill. Take a shower, honey, OK?

She reluctantly leaves. Silence.

HARRY (*quietly*). There maybe something in it.

WALTER (*pause*). Honest, Harry, this is the new poetry. And with your talent and connections –

HARRY. Connections?

WALTER. I figured if maybe you talked to your family –

HARRY. My family?

WALTER. The Morgans were one of the few to survive the Crash, weren't they?

HARRY. Survive? (*Nods.*) Not all. (*Pause.*) My Uncle Charles. You ever meet my Uncle Charles? (WALTER *shakes his head.*) Never had much time for my Uncle Charles. Always reckoned he was dead from the neck down. And on top all he had was a Burroughs calculator. Strange you can be so wrong. Apparently, as myth has it, everybody charging round him on the market floor as they claw down the cliff side, he leaves, strolls down Wall Street, into the block, nods at the porter whose name he was never to remember, up the elevator, outer office, ignored his secretary as was his custom, leather bound office, Uncle Charlie on the door, Yale photos of his football teams, his dying buddies, and up and out on to the window.(*He stands on the edge of the bed.*) Hell. What a view. Can you imagine the view?

WALTER. No.

HARRY. Come on, Walter, come and see the view. Don't be chicken. (*He drags* WALTER *up.*) Look down. See the well-heeled ants carrying home their dead from battle. You can make out ambulances, and crazies with red crosses on. What the shit are they doing? Whoops. Steady yourself. Old Charlie hasn't decided for certain yet. Down don't look too inviting. Then look up. It's October. The Fall. Grey clouds looming, the scrapers push upwards, ever upwards, fighting their way through them to the sun. And Charlie sees he is part of those scrapers, more than he was part of any family. In that moment, Charlie knows the clouds are just a thin sheet, veil we hide under. Let's fly through them. Fly out over the lady in the bay who holds high her torch not to light the weak and lonely but to signal to her Lord, the sun. What if it takes only this act of courage to be a god? Hold my hand. (*Pause.*) Hold my hand, Walter. What you frightened of, Walter?

WALTER. There's glass on the floor down there.

WALTER *climbs off the bed.*

HARRY. How can we make it together when you've no poetry in your soul, Walter?

ANGIE *enters.*

ANGIE. What is it?

HARRY. The film is over. Walter won't fly with me.

HARRY *climbs down.*

ANGIE (*quietly*). Shit. Shit, Walter, all shit.

WALTER (*long pause: then*). Let's go eat.

HARRY. There's food here.(*He kneels on the bed by the tray.*) Hell. No bananas. And my littl vierge expressly requested bananas.

WALTER. It doesn't matter.

HARRY. Of course it matters. It's what she wants. You want a banana more than anything els in the world, don't you?

ANGIE. Yes.

WALTER. I'll phone down.

HARRY. They obviously don't have any. Josephine Baker's got them all.

ANGIE. Try Les Halles.

WALTER. What?

HARRY. Great idea. That's where I got the flowers. Stacked up with bananas there. You pop down the market, and Louise and I can rehearse a little. See if there is still a possibility.

WALTER. Listen, I'm not going –

ANGIE. You won't go for me?

HARRY. She'll begin to think you don't love her.

WALTER (*softly*). There's no need to do this for me.

ANGIE. Do what?

WALTER. Harry. There's no need to do this to me.

HARRY. It always costs, Walter. You know that.

WALTER (*sharply*). I do. But you don't. Don't do this to me, Harry.

HARRY. It's only a film, pal. It's not real.

WALTER. Not to you. (*Silence: he picks up his coat, and, secretly, the gun, turning.*) I trust you, Harry.

HARRY. Why?

WALTER. Because I have no alternative.

HARRY. You must see that's your problem, not mine.

ANGIE. Walk, Walter. It's a beautiful night.

 ANGIE *smiles.* WALTER *leaves.*

HARRY. How do you feel?

ANGIE (*frowns*). Distante.

HARRY. Yes. It has that effect. Come closer.

 She moves over to sit by him. Her hand brushes his knee as she takes the book.

ANGIE. Is this the . . . script?

HARRY. Can't you read it?

 ANGIE *shakes her head.*

HARRY. Not even the name on the title page?

ANGIE. Harry Crosby. No. What do you call it?

HARRY. The Escaped Cock.

She smiles.

HARRY (*quietly*). This man feels dead. He meets a woman. She brings him back to life.

ANGIE. Is she dead also?

HARRY. Is she?

ANGIE (*pause*). Yes. I know this woman. You want I play her?

HARRY (*shivering: softly*). I don't want you to play. I'm sick of play. Sick of lies. I know you. Do you remember me?

ANGIE. No.

HARRY (*gently*). You really think the old life is left behind with the learning of a new language? You are still une belle de nuit. Une fille de joie. Une femme de Paris. A whore.

ANGIE (*pauses*). I am actress. (*Pause.*) I am film star.

HARRY. Let's face the truth together. Yes? (*Smiles.*) You'll never be a film star.

ANGIE. Walter promise when we get to America –

HARRY (*evenly*). There is no America. America is no more. Fini. Mort. America has fallen off the wall. The American dream of a New World out there has become just another lie. There's no life for you there.

ANGIE (*quietly, urgently*). I will be a star. Walter promise me.

HARRY. He lied to you.

ANGIE. Why would he lie to me?

HARRY. Because he loves you.

Silence.

ANGIE (*quietly*). Why are you so cruel?

HARRY. I don't know how to soften the truth, without distorting it.

She shivers.

ANGIE (*softly*). I'm so cold. (*Cries. Eventually.*). Help me. I can't stay here.

HARRY. I'll take you with me. We'll leave the corpse of Paris far behind, shake off the filth of Montparnasse, the fake imitation of the meeting ground of the gods, and sail away to an undiscovered country. But there is nowhere left on earth unexplored but in ourselves. 'O death, Old captain, it's time. Forward to the very bottom of the unknown to find the new.'

ANGIE. I don't understand the words.

HARRY.
O mort, vieux capitaine, il est temps! Levons l'ancre!
Au fond de l'inconnu pour trouver du nouveau.
Maintenant tu connais?

ANGIE. C'est la poesie, n'est-ce pas?

HARRY. Baudelaire. The words of a man who loved une femme de Paris.

ANGIE. You love me.

HARRY. But of course.

ANGIE. You are riche?

HARRY. Of course.

ANGIE. You take me to the new world?

HARRY. Of course. And you will bring me to life.

ANGIE (*smiling*). Of course.

HARRY. I knew. I knew you'd understand.

She embraces him.

ANGIE (*shivers*). I am cold.

HARRY. The sun will soon be out. Trust me.

She looks at him, quietly, then looks down at her red lingerie. She tilts her head, baffled, and places her hands on her heart. She stares at her hand. It's covered in blood.

ANGIE. No.

HARRY. Wait for me. Attend! Attend!

ANGIE. No. No. No.

HARRY. Don't say that. Please.

She tries to crawl away from him.

HARRY. Please, please understand.

Unable to speak she shakes her head before falling on the bed.

HARRY, *shaking, puts down the knife. He pulls the covers over her. He sits by her, wanting but not daring to touch her. He is having difficulty speaking. Band music from a party downstairs.*

HARRY (*softly*). So this is nausea. (*Sings*).
Even tho' my heart is broken
I always act gay
I just let them think I'm joking
It's better that way

My heart is aching
But no one will know
Clowning and joking
is the way I go

I'm all dressed up with a broken heart
just like an actor that plays a part
I'm playing the role of a Jekyll and Hyde
An unhappy soul
that keeps smiling outside
This world's a stage
and we're all in the show
There's no applause for the lower you know.
so with my chest up
I'll get all dressed up
The man with a broken heart.

He turns and moves to the edge of the balcony. As he opens it a blinding light cuts across the stage.

Blackout.

Scene Four

Le Prix de Beauté

As the shutter closes on HARRY *another opens on* ERIC, *with tray, his shadow cutting over the darkened bed. The Christmas tree is on the other side of the room, candles unlit. Silence.*

ERIC (*coughs politely*). Mam'selle. Votre peche, mam'selle. (*Pause.*) J'apporte votre peche que vous desirez. (*Sullenly.*) Don't pretend to be asleep just to do me out of my tip. I had to smash a grocer's window to get you this. (*Pause. Steps in the room, and closes the door. Louder.*) Mam'selle. (*Coughs again, this time it turns into a real coughing fit.*) Damn. Damn. Damn the lot of you. (*Places the tray by the bed.*) Here, I hope it chokes you. (*Stares at the figure in the bed.*) No, it can't be. Angie? Oh, God, so there is still someone who listens to prayers, who brings back traitors for justice. My little sleeping beauty. One kiss to show I can play Judas just as well as you.

He kisses her. She slowly wakes up, then, horrified, leaps out of bed on the verandah side.

That's no way out, mon petit chou. No, I'm the chou, aren't I? (*Slowly moving in on her.*) It's me you turned into a cabbage, me. Me you made the plat du jour. (*Reaching towards her.*) Well, bon appetit, mon amour. But now the bill of reckoning has come. (*She takes his hand and places it on her breast.*) No. No, that won't work any more my little angel. I'm impervious. (*She slides her hand down his body.*) Have you forgotten? I don't believe in resurrection. (*He shivers then looks down. Quietly.*) Oh. (*Stares at her: she smiles at him. With slowly dawning realisation.*) Did you know it was me? That's why you ordered the peach? You knew it was me, you've searched for me . . . to recompense me?

She leads him to the bed. He embraces her. She rolls on top, grabs the fruit knife and holds it to his throat.

Oh, no! Fou, Eric! Fou! Fou! Oh, Angie!

LOUISE (*desperately*). I'm not Angie.

ERIC. What's your name now?

LOUISE. Louise!

ERIC. Oh, yes. Go on, kill me, get it over with, Angie. Spare me at least a double shift.

LOUISE. Listen, I'm not your Angie. My name is Louise Brooks. I'm an American actress.

ERIC (*after long silence*). You're not Angie? (*Long pause.*) But . . . you look the spit of her.

LOUISE. I'm the spit of many women.

Silence.

ERIC. This is extremely embarrassing. (*Pause.*) I'm terribly sorry. (*Pause.*) I brought the peach you ordered.

LOUISE. You want I should say thank you?

ERIC. No need. Really.

LOUISE. Jesus.

ERIC (*after a pause*). I think I'd best be getting – (*Attempts to move.*)

LOUISE. Hold it!

She moves up his stomach. He groans.

LOUISE. I'm not sure I trust you. I've been stabbed to death once by a mad Englishman.

ERIC. Pardon?

LOUISE. Jack the Ripper when I tried to give him love for free.

ERIC (*confused*). Really?

LOUISE. It was in a film.

ERIC. Ah, yes, yes, of course. (*Pause.*) Afraid I haven't seen it. I don't go to the cinema much But I'll make sure to try to . . .

LOUISE (*sniffs the air*). What the hell's that smell?

ERIC (*pauses*). I'm not well.

LOUISE. My God!

She climbs off him, and opens the balcony shutters. ERIC *makes a move.*

LOUISE (*pointing the knife at him*). Don't you move!

ERIC *shakes his head, sits, knees up against his chest, on the bed.*

LOUISE. I'm still shaking. (*Pours a drink.*)

ERIC. I suppose this means you're going to report me?

LOUISE (*looks at him in disbelief*). You just tried to kill me?

ERIC. Not you.

LOUISE. It sure as hell felt like me.

ERIC. I can appreciate that, but it wasn't, it was really some completely different girl.

LOUISE. That supposed to make me feel better? (*Pause.*) What did this completely different girl do to you?

ERIC. She stole all my money.

LOUISE. That's a capital offence over here?

ERIC. No.

LOUISE. Just something worthy of revenge? Save your energy. Ten to one some other guy's already done the job for you.

ERIC. I wouldn't want that.

LOUISE. Don't want anyone else to get your fun for you?

ERIC (*simply*). I love her.

LOUISE. What the hell are you?

ERIC. My name is Eric. Eric Blair. (*Holds out his hand: she stares at it: he lets it drop.*) I'm a writer. Well . . . I came to Paris to write. But nobody wanted what I wrote, so I . . . I've given up. So you're an actress. (*Pauses.*) Angie wants to be an actress.

LOUISE (*pause*). Is she any good?

ERIC. She's a prostitute. I've never seen her act.

LOUISE. Haven't you? Sorry. I grow more cynical with each performance. (*She lights a cigarette.*)

ERIC. Are you good?

LOUISE. Didn't you rate me?

ERIC. Was that a performance?

LOUISE (*quietly*). Its gets increasingly difficult to tell. (*Shivers, pauses.*) In Berlin, I played a whore called Lulu. I stayed in a hotel laughingly called the Eden. The bar packed with girls selling themselves with strudel. I never saw a woman who wasn't a whore. Except for me of course. I only played one. (*Takes a drink.*) Best film I've ever made. No lies. Just nightmares and poisoned love all the way.

ERIC. What film was that?

LOUISE. Pandora's Box. Lift the lid of love and all the evils of the world are let loose. (*Pause.*) I don't want to be blown away.

ERIC (*pause*). Isn't there supposed to be something left inside the box?

LOUISE. What?

ERIC. Hope?

LOUISE (*quietly*). No one ever told me that.

She stares at ERIC. *He looks away, embarrassed. She slowly crosses to him, and sits by him. She hands him the knife.*

LOUISE (*softly*). Maybe I am your whore. (*Pause.*) Now what are you going to do?

ERIC. No, you're not. (*Pause.*) I'd better get back to the plates.

He rises. She lies back, eyes closed. ERIC *stops to look at her.* WALTER *enters.*

WALTER (*confused: misreading the scene*). Oh, gee, I'm sorry, I didn't mean to – (*Sees the knife in* ERIC'*s hand.*) What the . . . (*Draws out the gun.*) Hands up!

Totally terrified, ERIC *backs up and collides with the Christmas tree.*

LOUISE. Walter! What are you doing?

WALTER. This guy, this guy was about to kill you.

LOUISE. Don't be stupid, Walter. Put that gun away.

WALTER. He was standing over you with a knife.

LOUISE. I asked him to peel my peach, is that a crime?

WALTER. What? Oh, god, sorry. It's just . . . he was in here so long that I –

LOUISE. What the hell are you doing, watching my room?

WALTER (*evasive*). Poor guy. Look at him.

LOUISE. Leave him be. He's happy. He's a masochist.

WALTER. Come on, Louise. Don't be so cold. Pardon, monsieur, Let me . . . assistance.

He reaches out to take ERIC'*s hand to pull him up.* ERIC *screams.*

WALTER. He's got splinters in his hand. They could go septic. (*Signalling to* ERIC.) Septique! Get some hot water, Louise.

LOUISE. He's got pans of it downstairs. Let him go.

WALTER. Don't be so cruel.

LOUISE. You're the one wants to play Florence Nightingale. (*Nods.*) Through there.

WALTER *exits.*

ERIC. I'll just . . .

He attempts to resurrect the tree.

LOUISE. Leave it! Just leave it. I'll call the night porter.

ERIC (*lamely*). I am the night porter.

LOUISE (*sighs*). Merry Christmas, world.

WALTER *comes back with the bowl.*

WALTER. Assied! Assied!

ERIC *perches on the end of the bed.*

WALTER. Le main!

He takes ERIC'*s hand and starts to pick the needles out.*

LOUISE. Good will to men, eh, Walter. I must phone down and see if they've got a spare nativity. What are you doing camped outside my door?

WALTER. You know about Crosby's suicide?

LOUISE. I don't want to know. I've been in Berlin. I've seen enough killing.

WALTER (*pause*). How's La Prix de Beauté getting on?

LOUISE. Le film est fini.

WALTER. So you're set to go back home, then? (*She does not reply.*) They'll be glad to see you.

LOUISE. You want a bet?

WALTER. Sure.

LOUISE. What have you heard, Walter? What have the big boys said?

WALTER. Just they need you to dub the Canary Murder Case.

LOUISE. I don't know that I care for talkies, Walter.

WALTER. Silent movies are dead.

LOUISE. Don't call them silent movies, Walter, they're dance movies, dance movies the whole world could join in. The universal language, wasn't it you who called them that?

WALTER. Whatever you call them they're dead, Louise.

LOUISE. Twenty odd years, is that all we get before the world is sliced up with words again?

WALTER. But it's our words that are going to win.

LOUISE. You into competition now, Walter?

WALTER. We all have to face reality, Louise.

LOUISE (*turning away: picking out a few steps*). I'm not sure I want to give up dancing, Walter.

WALTER. Come on, Louise, be serious. You're not going to walk away from all the power they've given you.

LOUISE. What power? The power to have maniacs on both sides of the lights coming at you with a knife, or a gun? It no longer sounds like fun.

WALTER *plunges* ERIC'*s hands into the boiling water.* ERIC *groans.* WALTER *crosses to* LOUISE.

WALTER (*pause*). Louise, I'm . . . I can't pay the hotel bill, I can't . . . They offered to bail me out if I persuaded you to . . .

LOUISE. Oh, Walter. Walter.

WALTER. I'm sorry, but you're my last hope. (*Pause.*) What do you want, you want I take this gun and blow myself away?

LOUISE. You're not going to kill yourself. You're just going to wash a few plates. Ain't so bad. Is it, Eric?

ERIC (*looks up: sighs*). Well, the men are all right.

WALTER. Pardon?

LOUISE. Comradeship. That's what you're missing.

WALTER. I thought you were French?

ERIC. No.

WALTER. You mean you've been sitting there listening in on our private conversation?

ERIC (*pause*). Yes.

WALTER. Well, don't you think that's disgusting?

ERIC (*pause*). Sorry.

LOUISE. Don't apologise, Eric. The man's a writer. What else do you expect him to do? Tell him what's it like down there, Eric. (*Lights the candles.*)

ERIC. They cook you. One day your name comes up on the menu and you get to be the main course.

WALTER. Why do you stay?

LOUISE. Maybe he figures that's better than being one of the cannibals.

ERIC *turns to look at her.*

WALTER. Louise, you've gotta do this for me.

LOUISE. Why?

WALTER. Solidarity. We artists have to keep each other alive. Nobody else cares.

LOUISE (*pauses*). I feel sick, Walter. It's very strange, but I feel really sick. I don't want the part, Walter. I really, really don't.

WALTER. What's to happen to me then?

LOUISE. Wash up, or end up washed up, it's nothing to do with me, Walter. I'm tired, and I'm suddenly angry, and that's my sole responsibility. (*Looks up at the angel on the tree.*) Doesn't she look lovely? (*Pause.*) Good night, mon ami.

WALTER (*pause*). I loved you.

LOUISE. Or someone who was the spit of me.

WALTER *leaves.*

LOUISE (*puts her hand on her stomach*). Maybe I'm just hungry. (*She picks up the knife: turns to* ERIC.) Are you?

ERIC. No, thank you.

LOUISE. Let's not stand on formality. After all, you just tried to kill me. That suggests a certain level of intimacy.

ERIC (*nods*). Thank you.

LOUISE (*cutting peach in half*). Ibsen reckons we're all onions. Peel the skins away and there's nothing there. Well, he might be, but I'm a peach. (*Smiles.*) And what are you, Eric*

ERIC. I wish I knew.

She hands him the peach. He eats it ravenously. Dawn is rising.

LOUISE. Do I taste good? (ERIC *splutters.*) Don't be embarrassed, Eric. Apparently I've been eating you for weeks. It makes us equal. (*Pause.*) You tasted lousy.

ERIC. I'm not well.

LOUISE. So what you going to do about that?

ERIC. We fight back.

LOUISE. What do you do, spit in the soup? (*Pause.*) Is that the best you have at the bottom of your box, Eric?

ERIC. I want to write (*Pause.*) the truth but . . . I want to write, but . . .

LOUISE. But what?

ERIC. What are you going to do now?

LOUISE. The night I left Berlin, the director took my arm. I figured it was going to be a kiss and a gentle auf wiedersein, his words blistered my face. He said, 'Your life's exactly like Lulu's, and you will end up just the same.' (*Pause.*) I could have killed him. I'd sweated blood for his terrible, beautiful film, and now all he had to give was his anger. It has taken tonight to make me see. (*Pause.*) It wasn't an anger at me, so much as . . . for me. Anger with a world that did not value me. (*Silence.*) Who are you angry with, Eric?

ERIC *frowns.*

Maybe you and Angie have a lot in common?

ERIC. Except love.

LOUISE. You sure she didn't love you?

ERIC. That would be a nightmare. What do you call it, a nightmare of poisoned love.

LOUISE. Aren't you confusing nightmares with reality? Come on, Eric, if the world is poisoning you and yours, at least scream out.

ERIC (*pause*). Are you going to scream out?

LOUISE. The screams they want of women are quite a different thing. I'll do it in silence. (ERIC *nods. She turns to hear the band playing.*) Who's partying at this hour?

ERIC. It's the waiters. They feed the band. They dance. It's the only time they have.

LOUISE. Do you dance with them, Eric?

ERIC *shakes his head.*

LOUISE. Why not?

ERIC. I can't dance.

LOUISE. Anyone can dance. It just takes courage. (*Holds out her hand to him.*) Come on,
Eric. I don't want to dance alone. I'll give you a big tip.

ERIC. I couldn't do anything like that.

LOUISE (*laughs*). Don't be a fool for ever, Eric. Come on, be a peach.
*He slowly joins in her in the dance. The gold red of the dawn sun illumines the space, slowly
revealing the* WAITERS, *tired, stretching, and the* OLD COUPLE *who sing very gently –*

Life is just a bowl of cherries
Don't make it serious
Life's too mysterious
You work your play you worry so
But you can't take your dough
When you go go go

The WAITERS *sway with their bowls.*

So keep on repeating
Honey, it's the berries
And the strongest oak must fall

The sweet things in life
To you are just loaned
So how can you lose
What you've never owned?
Life is just a bowl of cherries
So live and laugh at it all

The OLD COUPLE *sing in French.*

La vie c'est rien qu'un bol de cerises,
Prêne pas un sérieux
C'est trop mysterieux
Travail, soucis, toujours comme ça
On ne prends pas les francs
Quand on va, va, va.

The dance finishes. Silence.

ERIC *and* LOUISE *part. He collects the tray. She places money on it, and moves off to take
down the angel from the Christmas tree. Without looking at* ERIC, *she goes to the balcony.
As the lights fade,* ERIC *takes the money off the tray and puts it in his pocket. He looks up to
see the watching* WAITERS. *He nods. Fade to blackout.*

Song Copyright

TIBETAN INROADS

To Mike W. and Bill G.
for an act each that could not have been written without them

Tibetan Inroads was first performed at the Royal Court Theatre, London, on 29 September 1981, with the following cast:

DORJE, a blacksmith	Kenneth Cranham
GENYEN, Jamyang's wife	Sharon Duce
TASHI, a monk, Dorje's brother	Mark Wingett
ABBOT	Fred Pearson
MOTHER, of Dorje and Tashi	Carmel McSharry
NEIGHBOUR	Sharman Macdonald
SINGER, her daughter	Madeline Church
BEGGAR	Phil Daniels
JAMYANG, a landlord	Paul Brooke
CHONGUP ⎫ brigands	Phil Daniels
PASANG ⎭	Fred Pearson
WIFE, of the brigands	Sharman Macdonald
TWO WHORES	Carmel McSharry
	Madeline Church
KASHOG	Paul Brooke
TUNG, PLA radio operator	Fred Pearson
SHAI, PLA propaganda officer	Sharman Macdonald
CHANG, PLA 'barefoot doctor'	Madeline Church
TONDRUP, a young monk	Phil Daniels
SURVEYOR, PLA	Paul Brooke
OTHER Parts	Colm Daly

Directed by William Gaskill
Designed by Roger Bourke
Lighting by Jack Raby

An earlier version was performed by students of Dartington College of Arts' theatre department in February, 1980.

My thanks to the actors and production team, especially those in the original workshop: Guy Roderick, Debbie Levy, Mike Hulls, David Hynes, Diana Howlett, Sian Webber, Bush Hartshorn, Katherine Cole, Rupert Button and Rosamund North.

And to Steve Paxton for choreography, Roger Bourke for design, and to my co-director, Joe Richards, and Graham Green – especial thanks to the last two for coping with me on our research trip into the Himalayas.

Tibetan Inroads was performed by Troupe on 29 February 1984 as part of the 1984 Adelaide Festival.

A note on the religion of Tibet

Buddhism, first introduced to Tibet in the seventh century A.D., replaced a shamanic religion, Bon, or Bonpo, which continued to survive in the hands of magicians and sorcerers. Even then much of the teachings of Bon were absorbed into Buddhist rituals, alongside Yoga, Tantric and Hindu practices.

In 1475 the leader of the Golugpa sect, Ngawang Lobsang, conferred on himself the title of the Fifth Dalai Lama (retrospectively establishing the four previous leaders of the order as his earlier reincarnations). Religious and secular rule was fused under his theocracy and reincarnation was established as an absolute doctrine.

The most famous Dalai Lama was the Sixth, Tshangyang-gyatso, who, until he was assassinated as a young man, achieved notoriety by frequenting brothels and composing popular love songs. The Fourteenth Dalai Lama fled to India in 1959. At that time it is estimated that one in three of the male population were monks.

The Bardo

With the doctrine of reincarnation the reading of the Book of the Dead (Bardo) became a central Tibetan ritual. Recited over the dead by lamas and paid for by the family, its intention is to free the soul from the wheel of life, or failing that, facilitate a better re-birth. There are seven descending levels to rebirth, if enlightenment is not secured.

One: At the moment of death there is the brief instant of luminous radiance – the 'light of Buddha'. The soul must try to submerge itself into this giving up all attachment to the illusory ego. Should it fail:

Two: The soul returns to the image of its former life. The aim is to perceive this as mere illusion and to regard one's past impartially.

Three: For seven days Buddhas and Bodhisattvas appear. They must not be feared or desired but prayed to with intense faith and humility. Should the prayers fail to release the soul:

Four: The same figures appear as angry deities. These are to be understood as reflections of the conflicts of the soul.

Five: Yama, the King of the Dead, the judge, holds up the shining mirror of Karma, where all past deeds are reflected.

Six: Depending on its Karmic state it then resides for a time in the lights of one of the six spheres; white/heaven, red/war, blue/a human being, green/animals, dull yellow/ghosts and darkish smoke/the hells.

Seven: The desire for rebirth is urgent; everywhere are animals and humans in the act of sexual intercourse. If, at this last stage, detachment is not reached, the soul will be absorbed into the act, and enter rebirth as a human being or an animal.

If the Bardo is not performed, or if the weight of Karma renders the journey unsuccessful, the soul may be re-born at a lower level of life.

In the sixteenth century, Tibetan 'Opera' began, initiated by a wandering group of players who were paid in food, drink and chains

Pontifex *(a song)*
the poet and players
creators of theatre
for three days and nights
their shapes
performed the magic rites –
an oasis
in the years of the village.

dance and the demons
song and the fools
high speech of kings
whisperings of lovers
folk tales and coarse jokes
filled the empty space
at the heart of the valley.

asking only for chains in payment
for all the joy and instruction
(the ale and food
and the unforced love of women
was all part of the celebration).

travelling,
the troupe linked the chains
building their bridges
from peak to peak,
across the ravines
uniting valley to valley.

lamas and lovers
traders and brigands
all walked the way
of the builders of bridges

and the blacksmith
worked hard and long
beating out poems
on the chains of rocks.

An unspoken prologue

In Tibet,
Legends say,
Lamas sit,
And melt the snow around them.
And we take heat
to manufacture ice.

What spring do we wait for?
What do we pray will clear away the snow?
What fire
What sun
Do we pin our faith upon?
Our dream is dwindling –
Like an idle pattern traced in the ashes.
Clawmarks in a blizzard.

Once upon a time,
In a far off land,
There lived a man.
As the snow fell
Did he dream on
Some unknown spring?

ACT ONE

Scene One

Above the valley.
Bright sunlight.
DORJE, *a young Tibetan man, sits on the ground, sharpening a knife against a stone. In front of him, on a skin, are laid out other knives and simple farm tools.*
It is a hill top.
Far below him, the distant sounds of music and chanting. He listens. He loosens his tunic, and takes off his prayer beads, counts off a few and wraps them round his wrist. He returns to work.
GENYEN, *a young woman, enters quietly behind him. She stands, silently, watching him.*
A bird calls overhead.
She touches her left breast gently with her hand.
He laughs at the bird.
She gives an almost imperceptible cry.
DORJE *stands, and turns to her, holding the knife.*
Silence.

DORJE. Don't run away. It's a dangerous path for so fine a mare.

GENYEN. I follow a path I know well.

DORJE. And where's your rider?

GENYEN. The man who paid is in the market, making money.

DORJE. Old fool, to let his treasure run free in the mountains.

GENYEN. The ride's too high and hard for him.

DORJE. But the jewelled halter around your neck, does that not hold you back?

GENYEN. Another man made it. Perhaps he owns it. Who knows?

DORJE *moves close to her, and touches her necklace.*

DORJE. Let's not riddle away the hours, like the old, in dreams.

GENYEN. The old woman warned me of demons and raiders in the hills. Round the fire they whispered of savage satisfactions. And my blood froze like the waters in winter, waiting for the heat of the blacksmith's hand.

She kisses his hand, and places it on her breast.

Bite me. Hurt me. Leave your mark. When the old man comes in the dark, let me feel the heat of you burning on my breast. I love you. I want to eat you. Be a meal for you. Butcher. Blacksmith. Dorje. I am the same as you. Love me.

He loosens her top, and kisses her. He kneels in front of her, and she opens her wrap-around garment.

Light on a young monk, TASHI, *and his* ABBOT.

RITUAL QUESTIONING: *The* MONK, *stands over his* ABBOT, *who sits in the lotus position. As he answers the questions, he whirls his prayer beads, and slaps them into his hand, stamping his foot at the same time. The answers are automatic, but the two of them are gaining obvious pleasure from the exercise.*

ABBOT. According to Lord Buddha, which is more important, the mind, body, or speech?

TASHI. Mind, for body and speech are servants of the mind, master.

ABBOT. But does your mind exist or not?

TASHI. One cannot say, because it has no shape or colour.

ABBOT. What then of self? Is self permanent or impermanent?

TASHI. Impermanent, master.

ABBOT. And does impermanence lead to suffering, or ease?

TASHI. To suffering, master.

ABBOT. But is it then wise to think of the impermanent, as 'This is mine, I am this, this is myself'?

TASHI. No, master. All that should be seen for what it really is. 'All this is not mine, I am not this, this is not myself.'

ABBOT. How then does the learned disciple respond to such external forms?

TASHI. With disgust. Disgusted, he sheds his desires for such things.

ABBOT. What then sets him free?

TASHI. His dispassion sets him free, and then he knows he is liberated.

ABBOT. What then does he know?

TASHI. Birth is extinct, the holy life completed; what had to be done has been done, there is nothing further to do. So he wisely knows.

Silence. The ABBOT *smiles, and nods at* TASHI.

ABBOT. Formless contemplation of the land. Look out over the land below our monastery. You remember the procedure (TASHI *nods.*) Close your eyes.

TASHI *sits in meditation. The* ABBOT *leaves.*

Lights up to include the two lovers.
GENYEN *lies on* DORJE's *chest, her open garment forming a loose blanket over them. Sh leans over, picks up the knife and runs it lightly across his breast.*

GENYEN. When you kill a pig, what do you think of?

DORJE. Food.

GENYEN. I'm not hungry.

DORJE. Not now. Not for a few hours, perhaps . . . A day.

GENYEN. Then there's always a banquet with the butcher. (*Pause.*) They say it's a sin.

DORJE. What?

GENYEN. The eating of meat.

DORJE. But they all do it, Genyen. They spit as they pass my shop, but they are all glad of it.

GENYEN. My husband eats no meat.

DORJE *laughs.*

DORJE. But Jamyang buys the saddles made of leather. It's all the same. They won't let me dig in the earth for lead and iron, yet they hoard their gold and trinkets.

GENYEN. If you had owned land . . . (*Pause.*) The astrologers said it was a good marriage.

DORJE. But they were paid for by Jamyang.

GENYEN. You don't believe them?

DORJE. I don't know. If I had paid them . . . I own nothing, except the few hours we steal together. What do we carry down the hill?

GENYEN (*smiling*). Your smell. I live inside it, like inside a ghost, until the next time.

DORJE. No Chinese perfume.

GENYEN. I could live with sweat and smoke. You always know there's a fire there. (*Looking under the 'blanket'*.) Even when there's little else to show.

DORJE. Always keep the fire going. I know my trade.

GENYEN. No, Dorje, I must go. He'll be waiting.

DORJE. Yes.

They begin to dress each other, slowly, lazily.

DORJE. The snows come soon. Where will we go then?

GENYEN. We'll roll in it together, and melt it all around. We'd flood the village with our love. Then they'd respect us. We'd be a miracle, and they'd worship us with food and fire. And we'd live naked, like the hermits, above them all. Anyone upset us we'd flood the village with our hate.

DORJE. We could meet in the hermit's cave.

GENYEN. Wherever. It doesn't matter.

DORJE *begins to pack away his knives.* GENYEN *crouches by his side, and idly picks up loose stones and begins to pile them up. As this occurs, the* ABBOT *enters to* TASHI.

ABBOT. Did you see the land in your mind's eye?

TASHI. Yes.

ABBOT. And did you take the sky away?

TASHI. Yes.

ABBOT. And did you take the ground away?

TASHI. Yes.

ABBOT. And did you take the rocks away, one by one?

TASHI. Yes.

ABBOT. And were you left with one stone?

TASHI. Yes.

ABBOT. And did you crush the stone to fine powder?

TASHI. Yes.

ABBOT. And did the wind blow away the powder?

TASHI. Yes.

ABBOT. And then what was left?

TASHI. Then?

ABBOT. What is left?

TASHI (reluctantly). One grain of dust.

ABBOT. Enough. Open your eyes.

TASHI *opens his eyes. The* ABBOT *stands quietly by him.*

DORJE. Who's it for?

GENYEN. I am building the shrine for the two demon lovers who live in this place. It's a famous legend.

DORJE. Is it?

GENYEN. Well, it will be.

DORJE. Do they haunt here?

GENYEN. Oh, no. They live here. But they haunt the valley below, looking for a glimpse of each other, waiting for the time they can be back here together. People fear them, but they're beautiful demons.

He kisses her gently. He looks away. She goes quickly. He turns around, sees she's gone, and quietly lays a few more stones on the pile. He finishes wrapping up his tools, and stands.

ABBOT. Where is your home, Tashi?

TASHI. My home is in the jewel in the centre of the lotus, and nowhere else.

The ABBOT *frowns.*

Is that not right?

ABBOT. It's no time for parrots.

Silence.

TASHI. Then my home is here, with you and my brothers.

ABBOT. Where is your family?

TASHI (desperately). Here.

ABBOT. What of the family you were born into? Your brother, and your mother, who still give you what they can ill afford to keep you here. You haven't come here, secure, with th riches of the world. You have had to work for wealthier monks to pay for your lodgings. B your food still comes up from the village. You rely on the world out there.

TASHI. I don't understand, master.

ABBOT. A monastery is no different from a monk. It, too, needs its food. At times, it begs. A other times, it wields its power.

TASHI. Power?

ABBOT. The Dalai Lama is both spiritual and temporal head of our land.

TASHI. Yes.

ABBOT. I, in turn, am both spiritual and temporal head of this valley. You follow?

TASHI. Yes.

ABBOT. Have you considered what temporal power means?

TASHI. No.

ABBOT. Look across the valley. We own half of all that harvest. It is worked by our serfs. And that power feeds us, provides for us, demands responsibility. We have to take actions, pass judgements, to keep the house in working order. Can all the monks wall themselves in for lengthy meditations at the same time? How long would those walls last? Who would mend them? Who would grow even the handful of barley we need for our tsampa? Who would make the cloth for our robes to keep us warm?

Silence.

The world is not so easily pushed away. I have a task for you in the village.

They go.

As the scene changes, and the village life begins, the GIRL *sings.*

A *Love Song of the Sixth Dalai Lama*

My love, to you my heart sails out
If we could only wed
Then I'd have drawn the greatest pearl
From the deepest ocean's bed.

High on the peach tree out of reach
The ripest fruit hangs there.
So, too, is the maid of noble blood
So full of life, so fair.

My love's far off, the nights drag by
In sleeplessness, in strife,
And morn brings not my heart's desire,
For lifeless is my life.

I dwell apart from men,
A God on earth am I
But hidden by the dark
I play the brigands king
In the brothels of desire

Lend me your wings, O whitest crane,
I go no farther
Than the yellow house
And then return again.

Scene Two

The village street
DORJE's *shop on one side. On the other, the* NEIGHBOUR *and the* GIRL, *her daughter, are setting out a limited supply of vegetables for sale.* DORJE *and his* MOTHER *are at work. A blind* BEGGAR *sits at the end with his bowl outstretched.*

MOTHER. Where did an innocent young girl pick up a song like that?

GIRL. It's a love s-s-s-song (*Stutters.*) by the s-s-s –

MOTHER. I know it's a love song. I'm not that old.

GIRL. Sixth Dalai Lama.

MOTHER. Oh well, if it's by the Sixth. Yes, well we old, we know about the Sixth. But what do you know about him?

GIRL. He wrote s-s-songs.

MOTHER. That's not all he did.

DORJE. Don't make the child blush, mother.

NEIGHBOUR. You're not blushing, are you?

GIRL. I'm not b-blushing.

DORJE. No.

MOTHER. As long as she doesn't understand what she is singing about.

NEIGHBOUR. She only stumbles when she talks. Not that she says much.

MOTHER. No disadvantage. A man doesn't want a nightingale to talk as long as she sings in her cage.

NEIGHBOUR. They say those houses the Sixth frequented in Lhasa –

MOTHER. What houses?

NEIGHBOUR. Those houses where young girls live. You know.

MOTHER. Oh, yes. Those houses.

NEIGHBOUR. They say, they are still painted yellow in his honour.

MOTHER (*laughing*). He had the passion of a man as well as a saint. (*To* DORJE.) Not that I want you taking after him. End up poisoned by the Chinese before your youth's flown.

DORJE (*laughing*). Don't worry, mother.

MOTHER. I worry about everything. Does a young girl good to blush. Finds the heart in a young man. They should both blush when they catch each other's eye. I bet there's a bit of red in your cheeks now, under all that smoke.

DORJE. If there is, it's only the heat from the furnace.

MOTHER. Shame on you. Shame.

She crosses over to her NEIGHBOUR. *The three women are eating from small wooden bowls. As she talks the* NEIGHBOUR *automatically places some food in the* BEGGAR's *bowl, which he eats slowly, before holding the bowl out again. When she finishes, she returns automatically to turning her prayer wheel.*

MOTHER (*to* NEIGHBOUR). I think he does like her.

DORJE (*amused*). What are the old hens hatching?

MOTHER. Old. That's right. You think about that. I can't go on fetching and carrying. I need time to rest my back and think of death.

DORJE. Mother, you sing the same song over and over.

MOTHER. Then why not a new singer?

DORJE. I'm used to the tune.

MOTHER. We need another pair of hands. To draw the water. Stoke the furnace. Hold the back legs of the pigs in the outhouse. All my life. Think of your poor mother. Think of the money we might make. Think of strong limbs.

The NEIGHBOUR *laughs.*

DORJE. Who would want a blacksmith, mother?

MOTHER (*to* GIRL). You think somebody might want him, don't you?

GIRL. I'm s-s-s-sure they w-

MOTHER. There you see.

NEIGHBOUR. He's charms enough to sell.

GENYEN *enters*.

MOTHER. Sell what you have, lad. You're a trader, not a monk.

DORJE. Let it rest, mother. We have business.

MOTHER. I'm talking business. It's my business as well. We need a woman. Many a girl without fancy ideas would be willing, wouldn't they?

DORJE. Can I help?

GIRL. I'm s-s-s-sure they –

NEIGHBOUR. She's sure they would.

GENYEN. I need to talk.

DORJE. This afternoon?

GENYEN. No. Now.

MOTHER. Dorje, you come sit down. Take your meal. Joke with your neighbours. I'll serve the fine lady.

GENYEN. Take the mare, now. Into the hills.

MOTHER. My son works too hard, Genyen. No wife to take the weight. How is your husband?

GENYEN. He's . . . well.

MOTHER. A fine man. A fine marriage. For you both. All marriages are fine. I believe in them all. Sit down, Dorje. I'll see to our old friend.

DORJE. Mother –

MOTHER. I do believe he's blushing. That's not the heat from the furnace.

NEIGHBOUR (*to* GIRL). Don't be shy.

DORJE. Mother, please.

GENYEN. I need your son –

MOTHER. We married women know of love. Let us have some joy in it. Seeing the children play.

DORJE. I'm not a child, mother.

MOTHER. Nor a married man either. Not yet.

GENYEN. I need your son to come see my horse.

DORJE. What is it?

GENYEN. I don't know. I'm not sure. I want you to ride it for me. Take it up to the pastures.

MOTHER. You want my son to ride your horse? What would people think? Is it sick? We know nothing of sick horses.

GENYEN. No. No. It's the bridle and halter that he made. I think it is too tight. It may be choking her.

MOTHER. Well, not so urgent. Let the lad eat and joke with his friend. Then you harness the mare and bring it here.

DORJE. I think I should go, mother.

MOTHER. He's just looking for an escape. But he doesn't really want one. Like all men. I'll trade with you. Eat and then go. One customer at a time. An extra pair of hands now will bring in gold. And when I'm dead it'll pay for the monks to say the whole Bardo over me before they feed me to the birds. I need the Lama's help so I'm not reborn as a blacksmith's wife. I deserve better than that.

TASHI *enters*.

NEIGHBOUR. And here's the man to make your dreams come true.

MOTHER. Tashi!

NEIGHBOUR. He'll give you the rites at a small price.

MOTHER. Dorje, fetch your brother food.

NEIGHBOUR. He'll pray hard to bring you back into a rich family, with pots of gold, who will feed you tsampa from a china bowl.

DORJE *goes*.

GENYEN. No.

MOTHER (*to* GENYEN). Tashi, my younger son. He can read and write. Genyen, the wife o Jamyang, the landowner. (*Crosses to* NEIGHBOUR.) This is worth a song, surely?

GIRL. I only know l-l-l-love songs.

TASHI (*quietly, sternly – to* GENYEN). Go. Your husband is kind. You are lucky not to feel the knife slit your nose. You can do nothing here. Leave us. Now.

GENYEN *leaves*.

MOTHER (*as she goes*). I'll send the lad this afternoon.

NEIGHBOUR. How do things look from up the mountain?

TASHI. The same.

NEIGHBOUR. You are like eagles up there. We mice still scurry around.

MOTHER. Looking for cheese as always.

DORJE *enters*.

DORJE. Where is Genyen?

TASHI. Gone to her husband.

DORJE. Where's your bowl, brother?

TASHI *takes his hand from within his robes. He holds out ankle-chains and padlocks.* DORJE *takes them.*

What's this mother? At long last the son brings the harvest back. So much food goes up the hill, but now the monk brings work down.

MOTHER. You'll stay a few days?

TASHI. No. I have other duties.

DORJE. There's nothing wrong with these chains.

TASHI. Our grandfather made them.

DORJE (*admiringly*). If I could do half so good. Chinese lock. Simple but strong. Is it broken? Where is the key?

TASHI. I have it.

DORJE. Give it to me. Let me see what I can do.

TASHI. The lock is good.

DORJE. I don't understand, brother. Is this some riddle they teach on the hill?

TASHI. There is no riddle, Dorje.

DORJE. Well?

TASHI. You are to accompany me to the monastery.

  Silence.

DORJE. The monastery? For work? Why the chains?

MOTHER. Come on, Tashi. Smile. Even a monk laughs. What is the game?

TASHI. No game, mother. Dorje must put on the chains and walk the hill. He goes for trial.

  Silence.

MOTHER. What have you done?

DORJE. I don't know.

MOTHER. What has he done?

TASHI (*pauses*). Put them on. Let's not make this time last any longer than it has to.

MOTHER. It can't be anything that deserves you drag him through the streets, like a criminal. A misunderstanding. Something said to a landlord after a few drinks. Smoke without fire. A child being a fool.

DORJE. Let me put the chains on at the edge of the village.

TASHI. What if you run away? I spend my life in meditation, not running the hills. Who would catch you there? Here, before you've run as far as I can throw a rock, my cries would have surrounded you.

MOTHER. I'll come with you. Neighbour, keep the furnaces going.

TASHI. Stay here. You'd only make things worse.

MOTHER. I'm his mother. How can I make things worse?

TASHI. Please. Put them on.

  DORJE *begins to fasten them.*

MOTHER. Let him go. Let him stand the cold of the snow on the mountain. By spring, the wind will have blown all trace of this away.

TASHI. I wish I could.

MOTHER. You can. Why do you think the Abbot sent you? His brother. Because he's giving us a chance. – It's a sign from Chenresig, our Lord of Compassion.

TASHI. Could that be?

MOTHER. Of course. What else could it be?

TASHI *stands, uncertain.*

MOTHER. I beg you. Tell him, neighbour. Tell him of the prayers we spin a day; the endless counting of the hundred and eight beads. Tell him.

NEIGHBOUR. We don't know what the crime is.

MOTHER. We don't need to know to give mercy.

TASHI. No, mother. I have been sent to understand my duty. It's a test for me, and if I fail, I fail you and all my teachers.

He kneels to check the chains.

MOTHER. You have failed me already.

TASHI. There are things that happen behind those walls that you can never understand.

MOTHER (*angrily*). Nothing happens behind those walls that an old woman can't understand.

DORJE. It needs the key to lock it.

TASHI *locks it.*

MOTHER. Tashi. When your brother drags his feet through the streets for all to mock and spit on, don't think that he has brought shame to our family. It's not the son in chains who has done that.

DORJE. It's nothing. Mother. I'll be back. Stay here.

He begins to walk off. TASHI *follows him.*

NEIGHBOUR. I will pray for your family.

MOTHER. Pray for what?

NEIGHBOUR. Wait until the fire goes out. Then you'll see it more clearly.

MOTHER. The fire never goes out. Not in my house. Never.

Blackout.

The GIRL *sings*

My love's far off, the nights drag by
In sleeplessness, and strife
And morn brings not my heart's desire
For lifeless is my life

Scene Three

The Monastery.
The ABBOT *sits on cushions, raised high. Behind him is a large mandala of the wheel of life.*
JAMYANG, *a middle-aged man, stands to one side of him.*
DORJE *kneels in front of them, his feet chained.*
MONKS *sit around the edge of the area. As the light comes up,* TASHI *stands by* DORJE. *The* ABBOT *nods at him and he takes his place alongside the other monks.*

ABBOT. Lord Jamyang, do you still wish to accuse?

JAMYANG. I do, Rinpoche.

ABBOT. Speak.

JAMYANG. I wish to accuse this man of stealing my wife in adultery.

ABBOT. And?

JAMYANG. And, Rinpoche?

ABBOT. I would have thought that you, as a secular magistrate, would be familiar with the procedure.

JAMYANG. And I beg for justice, Rinpoche.

ABBOT. Dorje, do you deny or affirm the charge?

DORJE *is unable to speak.*

ABBOT. Do you understand me?

DORJE *shakes his head.*

ABBOT. Jamyang accuses you of carnal knowledge of his wife. Help him, Tashi, he needs to speak. Speak to him. Make him understand.

TASHI. Dorje, have you made love to Genyen?

DORJE *nods.*

ABBOT. Since she became the wife of Lord Jamyang?

He nods again.

JAMYANG. She has confessed it anyway, Rinpoche.

ABBOT. So I understand. Nevertheless, an honest admission is worth something (*Pause.*) What more do you want?

JAMYANG. I want justice, according to tradition.

ABBOT. Take all his property, confiscate.

JAMYANG. My lord, he has no land. He is a blacksmith, a butcher. A slayer of pigs. He has little I want, that could pay the price.

ABBOT. What then?

JAMYANG. Only justice.

ABBOT. Dorje, do you confess your sin? Do you see the illusion of that path you follow? It leads only into darkness and despair. Swear that you will break from this path, and return to the only true way.

DORJE *mumbles something.*

ABBOT. What did he say?

TASHI. Nothing, my lord.

ABBOT. What did he say, Tashi?

TASHI. He said the woman's name, master.

JAMYANG. See Rinpoche. Even here, he incants her name, to chain her soul. He practises charms and spells. How else could the lowest bewitch the highest and drive her beyond her senses? I cannot have him free to make his magic as he desires.

ABBOT. Quiet. Dorje, swear that you will break from this path.

DORJE (*softly*). The Sixth.

ABBOT. What does he say?

TASHI (*shakes his head*). The Sixth. He just said the Sixth.

DORJE. The Sixth. Dalai Lama. He did as men do. Women. they sing songs of him. They praise him.

ABBOT (*sharply*). The Sixth! You dare to evoke the name of Tshangyang-gyatso, the Dalai Lama, in your defence? The demons have you. The esoteric meaning of that life is not for fools to play with. Your desires possess you and drive you mad. Jamyang, you have your way. I had hoped. Listen, Dorje, many reincarnations will depend on you understanding this. Do you hear me.

DORJE *nods*.

ABBOT. We of the Buddhist faith, brought to our land by the great Padmasambhava, we, of the Galek-pa order, we neither believe in revenge or retaliation. Only in certain closely defined circumstances can we inflict suffering on a wrong-doer. Only when it is clear that he will repeat the same error over and over again. And in so doing, will build such a great mountain for his karma that he will be crippled by its weight on his back for endless births, binding him fast to the wheel of Life. For his sake, we are allowed to do all in our power to restrain him. You have stolen a man's wife. Her name is still upon your lips and in your every thought. You defame the re-incarnations of the Dalai Lama himself in one of his holy places. You need to be freed of these desires that torment you. No other way but that of tradition can be taken. For your sake. The judgement: All that he owns to be confiscated to Jamyang, and the prisoner himself to be emasculated.

DORJE *does not respond*.

It is important that he understand. Lift his head up.

TASHI *does so*.

You are to be castrated.

DORJE (*almost incoherently*). No, you are mistaken, Rinpoche. Lord, I do that to animals. To horses. To rams, I don't do that to men. No. I see. Yes, forgive me. You are right. I see. Forgive me. I swear I'll never do it again. Yes, I see it's wrong. Not to any animal. I'll not take a knife to any animal. They are sacred, yes, I'll not slaughter or geld or eat any animal. It was all I was taught. It was wrong. Forgive me for being a butcher. Please.

ABBOT. He is raving. His desires blind him. We will open his eyes.

DORJE. Give me my knives. Let me do it. I am the butcher. I'll rip open the carcass and stop the heart, for the New Year's festival. Give me my knife.

ABBOT. We must all live with the consequence of our actions. It is the law of karma.

He rises.

Blackout.

Scene Four

The monastery's hospital.
A MONK lights a candle in front of statues of bodhisattvas. Above them, dimly seen in the candlelight are the signs of Om Mani Padme Om, in the colour sequence white/blue/yellow/green/red/black. The idols are each clothed in their respective colour. The GIRL sings.

Milarepa's song: I fear not

In fear of death I built a house
Now my house is the house of the great void
And I fear not death

The Candles reveal a small, cloth-latticed bed, on which DORJE *is lying, covered by a blanket. By the side of the bed is a small bowl of food.*

I am the sage who lives in the cave
Stocked high with the treasures of desire
But where e'er I live
I lie down my head
Contented.

Silence.
DORJE *jerks occasionally in his sleep. The shadowy figure of the* ABBOT *stands by him. A monastic ritual begins nearby, at first with soft chanting and then with music.*
TASHI *enters, with a bowl of food.*

TASHI (*surprised*). Rinpoche.

ABBOT. He sleeps. Leave the food.

TASHI. He must eat.

ABBOT. Let the fever run its course.

TASHI. His tongue rejects meat, with his eyes closed.

ABBOT. Our brothers feed him pills of herbs. As well as mercury, and gold.

TASHI. He'll live? Will his eyes open? Rinpoche?

ABBOT. As the suffering ebbs away.

   DORJE *begins to stir into life.*

DORJE (*screams*). No. Don't. Please.

TASHI (*quietly*). Brother.

DORJE. Where's the light? Have I missed the light? It says in the Bardo, after death, the light of Buddha, and then the slow darkness into rebirth. Don't cheat me of the light. Just one second. I've paid. Mercy (*He raises himself up*) Now. I see. Saints. Help. Where are the monks who read to me, tell me what to do? Who is reading the book of the dead? Please.

ABBOT. Speak to him. Explain.

TASHI. Brother – it's Tashi.

DORJE. Tashi . . . Read the words to me. Give me the wisdom for a good rebirth. I think I've missed the light of Buddha. But . . . Read the words.

TASHI. Dorje, don't fear.

DORJE. I can't hear you for the monks chanting. So many. Who is paying for all those monks? It's the Bardo of a prince. Do they pay? Those who wronged me to buy their way into nirvana. Let it work for me.

TASHI. Brother, you are still in this world. (*Pause.*) You are not dead.

DORJE (*crying out*). Why not?

   He lies face down on the bed.

ABBOT. Give him the teaching. Tashi. Now. He is your responsibility.

TASHI. Brother, you are not dead. You must carry the weight of your karma in this life. You are in the monastery's hospital. The saints you see are the images of the bodhisattvas, great doctors of the body and soul. They watch over you. See only them. Your way now lies with their guidance. I don't know if he understands me.

DORJE. Why am I not dead? You took my life from me. Why am I not dead?

TASHI. No one has taken your life. We give you life. You were blinded by the strongest desire that holds men to the material world. It's a stone you have carried through many lifetimes, until like the sage Milarepa your back was just one inflamed sore. We have lifted the rock. You are free of it. The traces of desire that still haunt you will soon fade away. Now accept t great gift. Give me a sign you are on the way. Eat, brother.

TASHI *places the bowl by him.* DORJE *slowly raises himself to a sitting position and takes up the bowl.*

A third, shadowy figure appears.

MOTHER. Son.

TASHI. Mother. How did you get here? Go. Now.

MOTHER. Let me see my son.

TASHI. It is not allowed. You can do no good.

MOTHER. What good have you done?

ABBOT. I leave you. Comfort him, Tashi. But remember his is a dangerous way. Hidden rocks can cut the feet even in the greenest meadow.

He leaves.

MOTHER. They gave me no time to bury anything. Even your knives, Dorje. They took your knives, the tools. I begged him, him who eats no meat, I begged him one thing, leave me the lamb. I won't slaughter it. It was marked for slaughter but let me put the red ribbon round it neck and free it according to custom, that no man will capture it, so my sick son can rise off his bed by the freeing of the lamb to the mountains. His men killed it in front of me with your knives.

TASHI. It's not the time for this. Let him eat. Let him turn his thoughts away.

MOTHER. Don't silence me. They left us nothing. Not even the freedom to starve. Jamyang claimed me as his serf. I am to carry his shit in broken buckets to the field. They take our future from us. Our children. They leave us no seed or even barren land!

DORJE *puts his face in his hands.*

TASHI. This is holy ground, mother. This is no place for hate.

MOTHER. That is all they have left us. Go, son, and come back with new knives. Find a man who will teach you how to slaughter men.

DORJE. Mother.

He kneels down on the floor in front of Buddha.

TASHI. Enough!

MOTHER. It will never be enough.

TASHI. Brother, don't listen. Hold only the face of Buddha before your eyes. There lies the way. Leave. Follow the path of the pilgrim until you meet your master. Look on the face of Buddha that you will recognise him. There lies true mercy. Not the mercy of men, but the freedom from suffering given only by Buddha.

MOTHER. Find a man who will teach you how to slaughter.

DORJE *looks up at the face of Buddha. The* GIRL *sings a song of the Sixth Dalai Lama.*

I went to my teacher, with devotion
To learn the way of the Lord Buddha
My teacher spoke, but words became smoke
And I saw the face of another
The compassionate one has stolen my mind
I see the face of my lover.

DORJE. Genyen.

Blackout.

Scene Five

The mountain.
White. Barren. Winter.
A small cairn with flag indicates the top of a pass.
A peasant woman – the WIFE *– enters, with baggage. She is exhausted and cold.* CHONGUP *and* PASANG, *dressed in furs and armed with long knives, follow her and collapse by her side.*

WIFE. Now where?

CHONGUP (*to PASANG*). Now where?

PASANG. Shut up.

WIFE. You knew the right way didn't you, husband? Just like you know where all the rich pickings are. All the others go off one way, but you have to drag us into the snow. They'll all be in Lhasa warming their bums by now.

PASANG. Tell our wife to shut up.

CHONGUP. Shut up, wife.

WIFE. Shut up yourself, husband.

Silence. The WIFE *begins counting her prayer beads.*

PASANG. Eat now.

CHONGUP. Good.

WIFE. No. If we eat now we'll be hungry later.

PASANG. I'm hungry now.

WIFE. Who knows how long its got to last us.

PASANG. One of these days wife . . .

WIFE. Don't give me the pleasure of telling *my* brothers. (*Pause.*) Let's go.

PASANG. Where?

WIFE. We'll leave you here for the birds if you like.

She starts off. The MEN *stagger up with their packs.*

PASANG (*to CHONGUP*). I could brain you, letting the mule die. I should have fed it your share. I wasn't thinking.

WIFE. There's somebody coming.

PASANG. I told you. Rich pickings. Didn't I say?

CHONGUP. You did.

PASANG. Hide. Quick. Before he runs away. Then we'll jump him as he passes.

CHONGUP. Good thinking.

WIFE. Where you going to hide? There's nothing but snow.

The MEN *begin to charge around, crazily. The* WIFE *stands watching them.*

PASANG. Yes.

CHONGUP. Yes.

PASANG. We'll pretend to be a couple of rocks.

WIFE. Don't strain yourselves. I'll distract him for you.

CHONGUP. Be a rock. Crouch down with your head between your legs. Then he'll not see We'll just be part of the mountain.

WIFE *sighs.*

The two men bend over.

PASANG. He'll never see us now.

WIFE. How you going to see him?

PASANG. What?

WIFE. Never mind.

CHONGUP. I feel dizzy.

DORJE *enters, head down, deep in thought. The* WIFE *stands, provocatively, in his way. He passes her without noticing.*

WIFE (*to herself*). I must be losing my touch.

DORJE *walks into CHONGUP. Both of them are terrified.*
DORJE *falls over.* PASANG *leaps round with his knife.*

CHONGUP (*screaming*). Kill him. He's got me.

PASANG *kicks* CHONGUP.

PASANG. Get up. What sort of brigand are you?

DORJE. Brigands?

PASANG. That's right, pilgrim. So don't play any games. The rest of our band is waiting behind the hill, just in case you manage to make a break for it.

DORJE (*terrified*). Where?

PASANG. Over there.

He and CHONGUP *point in opposite directions.*

PASANG. You're getting up my arse, brother.

WIFE. Yes, well, I'm getting frostbite in unusual places as well. So hurry up.

PASANG. Give us your offerings.

DORJE. What?

PASANG. Your rich jewels, and gold, for the temples.

DORJE. I don't have anything.

PASANG. You're lying.

DORJE. Nothing. They took everything I had.

WIFE. Just look at him. Rich, fat pilgrim.

PASANG. You're lying.

WIFE. He's not lying.

PASANG. You've swallowed them. You heard us, and you ate them.

WIFE. He's shit scared. If he'd swallowed anything it would be shining in the snow by now.

Silence.

PASANG. You've got a nerve, making us run around like this for nothing. It's the last time you'll waste an honest peasant's time.

He raises his sword.

WIFE. Don't get rust on your knife. Just take his food and clothes and let's get off.

PASANG. Get up.

DORJE *stands.*

PASANG. Get your clothes off.

DORJE (*pauses*). I'll freeze to death.

PASANG. Not you holy men.

DORJE. I'm not a holy man.

PASANG. They all say that, when you want something. But it's different when they pass the begging bowl.

CHONGUP. Pasang, him being a holy man. Perhaps he's . . .

PASANG. What?

CHONGUP. In front of our wife.

DORJE. Who's wife?

CHONGUP (*proudly*). He's my brother.

PASANG. Well, we might as well do it decent. Turn your back, woman.

CHONGUP. We're a decent family. I always turn my back when it's his turn with her. You never know what's happening.

PASANG. 'Cept you make so much noise.

CHONGUP. You make more than I do.

PASANG. No. I don't.

CHONGUP. No. No. She makes more than both of us.

WIFE. Only when I'm yawning. Come on. We won't be in Lhasa for the New Year at this rate.

PASANG. Give some respect woman. She won't look.

WIFE. Who says?

CHONGUP (*looking for* DORJE*'s bag*). He's hardly got a handful of tsampa.

WIFE. Rich pickings.

PASANG (*angry*). Come on. Now.

DORJE. I'll die. I don't want to die.

PASANG. Why not?

Silence

There you are, you see. Least this way you're being useful to your fellow man.

DORJE (*desperately*). I can be useful. I can be more useful than a few rags and a handful of tsampa.

PASANG. Oh yes, how?

DORJE. I could carry your bags so you could travel faster.

PASANG. There's a thought.

WIFE. I could use an extra body.

PASANG. Shut up, wife.

CHONGUP. Shut up, wife.

DORJE. And I was a blacksmith. I could fix your knives. I could make you new ones. And bracelets. I could make the fires. Do anything.

WIFE. We could do with all the help we can get. We're losing money wi' me not in the yellow house.

CHONGUP. We just lie down and rest but she lies down and gets paid. (*He laughs.*)

WIFE. It's his one joke.

DORJE. What?

WIFE. He's an innocent. Here, pick that up. I'm off.

PASANG. I'm thinking.

Silence

Go on then. But no funny business with our wife.

DORJE. I'm celibate.

Silence

PASANG. That makes no difference. No sharing the woman. She's got to keep us through the winter.

WIFE. Just my luck. I could have done with a change of diet.

CHONGUP *dumps his pack by* DORJE.

PASANG. He can't take yours.

CHONGUP. Why not?

PASANG. Who killed the mule?

CHONGUP *loads himself up.* PASANG *sets off in the direction* DORJE *came.*

DORJE. Lord.

PASANG. What?

DORJE. I came that way.

PASANG. So?

DORJE. I don't think Lhasa can be that way. That's south.

Silence

PASANG. I know that. I was just taking a last look at the valley.

CHONGUP. Why?

PASANG. Follow me.

He is about to go off in the direction they entered in, when he remembers and marches off in another. The rest follow him.

Blackout.

GIRL *(sings).*
I dwell apart from men
A God on earth am I
But hidden by the dark I play
The brigand king
In the brothels of desire.

Lend me your wings, O whitest crane
I go no further than the yellow house
And then return again.

Scene Six

A room in a Lhasa brothel.
At the centre of a small room is a low, square stone Tibetan fire with a hole in the top through which escapes the smoke of a slowly smouldering fire. Thin, single mattresses, one on each side, spread from it. The two GIRLS sit on the fire, warming themselves, and an old drunk, KASHOG, lies, unconscious, over it.
The WIFE enters first.

WIFE. Fire!

GIRL 1. Where you been? We'd given up hope.

WIFE. Been playing in the snow with them two. Give us an inch.

GIRL 2 *rolls* KASHOG *off, to provide space for the* WIFE. *She sits down.*

Aaaah. I've been dreamin' of this. Get me bum warm.

PASANG *enters, followed by* CHONGUP. *They are both drunk.*

PASANG. Greetings, lucky ladies.

GIRL 2. You haven't bought your husbands again.

WIFE. Don't think it gives me any pleasure.

GIRL 1. Why don't you just dump them?

WIFE. What, and get lumbered with them again in the next life. No, I'd rather pay now, and get it over with. I kept praying for an avalanche but it did no good.

PASANG. Celebrations. Party night. Pasang does it again.

CHONGUP. What?

PASANG. I said I'd get you to civilisation, didn't I? Not that anybody believed me.

CHONGUP. No.

PASANG. What?

CHONGUP. I believed you.

GIRL 1. They're going to be a load of fun.

WIFE. They hit the drink soon as they reached the first shack.

GIRL 2. Well, they won't tire us out.

WIFE. They wouldn't anyway.

DORJE *enters with baggage.*

PASANG. Where you been? Here, have a drink.

DORJE. No.

PASANG. Too holy for life you are. Be glad to be shut of you. Pain in the arse. Come on, who's fucking who? We men want livening' up an' all, you know.

WIFE. You want a raiser of the dead, not a woman.

KASHOG. What do you want? Love potions. Some'at to keep it up for days. Charms. Spells You name it. Give us a drink.

PASANG. Buy your own.

GIRL 1. Go back to sleep, Kashog. We're busy.

KASHOG. I was here first.

GIRL 1 *has taken an interest in* DORJE.

GIRL 2. Don't worry. I'll get another gal next door to come in for you lot.

GIRL 1. Who's this then?

GIRL 2. I was here first.

WIFE. Don't bother. He's a holy man.

GIRL 2. So?

KASHOG. So am I.

GIRL 2. And it dun't stop him.

WIFE. You won't tempt him. Believe me.

GIRL 2. Shame.

DORJE. Is there another room?

GIRL 1. Ye, but they might be worse than this. It's the New Year festival.

DORJE. I'll leave you then.

PASANG. Good riddance.

CHONGUP. Ye.

WIFE. Don't be daft. Everywhere's packed out, and if you try to sleep in the road, you'll wake up wi' your throat cut. You can hardly stand up as it is, wi' carrying all that stuff. Get to sleep and see what world you're up against in the morning.

GIRL 2. There'll be nothing goin' on here that would tempt a randy young clerk. Not with them in the condition they are in.

KASHOG. What's the complainin' about? This is a holy place. Perfect for holy men like you and me, son. The Sixth Dalai Lama slept here. That's the only reason I come.

WIFE. Go on. Lie down.

KASHOG. Holy. And it's a sight more laughs than the Potala, I can tell you.

WIFE. Go on.

GIRL 2 . Nobody'll rape you.

DORJE *lies down.*

PASANG. Right. No time like the present. Down to business.

WIFE. For some.

GIRL 1. Normal rates.

PASANG. On the house, surely?

GIRL 1. Don't be daft.

WIFE (*to* GIRL). Don't ask for miracles.

PASANG. Bloody whores.

KASHOG. Who's having who?

They stare at the women, who sit, with their backs to them.

CHONGUP. How many are there all together?

PASANG (*counting*). One. Two. Three. Four. Five . . . Enough.

CHONGUP. Can I have the one in the middle?

PASANG. Why?

CHONGUP. 'Cos all the others keep jumping about too much.

PASANG. I want the middle one.

CHONGUP. Why?

PASANG. Because . . . because if you want her, you must know some'at I don't know. And I'm first.

CHONGUP. I don't know nothing.

WIFE. Except she's your wife, you daft pair of fat yaks.

Silence. They study her.

PASANG (*to* KASHOG). You have her.

KASHOG. I don't care.

CHONGUP. I'll have the one that's left.

The women lie down on mattresses. The men walk round to their women.

PASANG. Here, come on.

GIRL 2. What?

PASANG. Get 'em off then.

GIRL 2. You takin' yours off, are you?

PASANG. What? And freeze me balls off.

GIRL 2. Ye, well, same for me.

CHONGUP. Yours an't got balls, 'as she?

PASANG. Shut up.

GIRL 2. I an't got all night you know.

The WIFE *laughs.*

PASANG. It in't fair.

GIRL 2. What is?

CHONGUP (*to* GIRL). You suit yourself.

KASHOG (*to* WIFE). I don't care.

WIFE. Good job.

The men join the women. GENYEN *enters, and kneels quietly on the edge of* DORJE's *mattress.*

GENYEN (*softly*). Dorje. Dorje.

DORJE (*in his sleep*). No. Don't touch me, lady. I'm not . . . Just leave me to sleep.

GENYEN. Dorje. Open your eyes.

DORJE. Leave me, please.

GENYEN. Open your eyes.

He sits up slightly.

DORJE. Genyen?

GENYEN. Yes.

DORJE. It can't be.

She smiles.

What are you . . . you shouldn't be here.

GENYEN. Softly. Your friends are sleeping.

DORJE. Not here. You shouldn't be . . . What happened? Did he throw you out? He must have given you money. No man could just . . . Don't tell me I brought you to this. I've paid enough. Not that, Genyen. Please.

GENYEN. I'd love you to weep on my breast. To hold you. I wanted beyond life itself to come to you. He locked me away. I pined to the point of death, Dorje. Dorje, listen to me carefully. I am still in that room.

DORJE. What are you talking about?

GENYEN. I am still in that room. Beyond the snow and the blocked passes. My real body, Dorje, is locked in another room.

DORJE. What are you saying?

GENYEN. One of those spirits on the hill, Dorje. She's lonely. And she's wandered a long way, looking.

Silence

DORJE (*quietly*). You're dead. They're reading the Bardo over you. You won't hear them here, Genyen. You'll hear no words of the lamas in the cries here. Don't give up Nirvana for me. I can give you nothing. Go back.

GENYEN (*laughing*). Oh, Dorje. I'm not dead. I've just searched you out in my soul. I'm haunted by the thought you might hate me.

DORJE. Hate you?

GENYEN. That I betrayed you. Perhaps I did. But I want your forgiveness. One night, in the dark, even his wildest imaginings did not feed him. He took a candle, and ran the light over my body, hoping to find a feeling flickering inside of him. But he only found your marks. He whipped me, like a broken horse, until I talked. Look.

She loosens her garment, which falls around her, and bends forward to show him her scarred back. DORJE *moves his hand over her back.*

DORJE. A man did this?

GENYEN. Yes.

DORJE. What are we men that we can cause such pain?

GENYEN. But another man made the marks upon my breast.

She sits up.

DORJE. I want to touch you.

GENYEN. It's no use. You can't.

DORJE. I know.

GENYEN. No. Not because of that.

DORJE. What's happening. Who are you? (*He runs his hand across his face.*) I'm burning. What are you? The monks told me, they've freed me of this. Where have you come from?

GENYEN. Dorje, please, listen.

DORJE. They said I'd never feel like this again. I can't do anything. I'm not a man. I can't feel like a man. That's the only way I can bear the weight. What magician has sent you? Has Jamyang followed me beyond the grave to haunt me with desires? No. I want to enter you. To join you. Devil. You've worked your magic. Go back to Jamyang. Let him laugh round the fire. You've brought me hell. I won't leave it now. Tell him, though. Even in that hell of endless fires, I'll search for revenge. I'll bring him here. I swear. Go back.

He rolls into a tight foetal ball. GENYEN *shakes her head.*

GENYEN. Don't close your eyes, Dorje. Let me stay a little. Don't send me back. Just yet.

She passes her hand above his body. He doesn't move. She covers herself, and slowly walks away. DORJE *moans, as though in sleep.* KASHOG *rises and touches* DORJE's *shoulder.*

DORJE. NO!

KASHOG. Quiet, boy. Or you'll have us all kicked out. Gently. It's over.

DORJE. It's not over.

KASHOG. You're sweating bad. You have a fever. Here.

He tries to cover him with a blanket.

DORJE. Give me a sword.

KASHOG. What for?

DORJE. I have to kill.

KASHOG. Yourself?

DORJE. I'm dead already. I have to kill the men who cast me into hell.

KASHOG. You're a boy. What do you know of hells?

DORJE. The sword.

KASHOG. There are better ways of killing than that.

DORJE. What do you mean?

KASHOG. Sleep. The festival gives everyone wild dreams. Sleep. In the morning you won' remember a thing. I never do.

DORJE. The brigands. They'll help. We'll loot the monastery together.

KASHOG. The monastery. Hadn't you better pick on something your own size?

DORJE. We'll make them pay.

KASHOG. This lot won't help you raid a monastery. They clip at the toenails of religion, that's all. You need other allies to take that on, and it takes more than a man whipped for stealing a handful of tsampa to control those powers.

DORJE. They castrated me.

Silence.

KASHOG. Sleep. We might talk in the morning. If you remember.

Blackout.

Scene Seven

The brothel.
Morning.
The noise of a New Year Festival outside. Shouting, yelling, music. DORJE *sits, watching th‹ sleeping* KASHOG. *The others have gone, but their possessions still lie around.* KASHOG *wakes, slowly, painfully. He starts when he sees* DORJE.

KASHOG. Frightened me to death.

DORJE. They say you are a magician.

KASHOG. They say. They say. Who are they? They don't know they are dead until a lama tells them so. (*Groans.*) I think I'm dying.

DORJE. You are a magician. I know you are.

KASHOG. Get lost. Have I missed the horse racing? I've me money to get down.

DORJE. A great magician.

KASHOG. Can't you see? I'm an old drunk in a whorehouse. Even pigs won't eat the shit when they see I've walked in it.

DORJE. It is the way of the master to pretend to be an ordinary man. I know the story of Milarepa and his teacher.

KASHOG *gets up and makes his way to a bucket.*

KASHOG. You're mad.

DORJE. Does that make any difference?

KASHOG *drops his pants and sits on the bucket.*

KASHOG. Will you stop watching me? It's not turned you into a woman, has it?

DORJE. No.

KASHOG. Mind you, even if it had you wouldn't fancy me. They never do.

DORJE. I want your knowledge.

KASHOG. Want. Want. I want a shit, but you're putting me off. Even if I was one of these magicians why should I give my magic to you?

DORJE. Because I need it. I need the power to make them suffer. It's the only thing to satisfy me.

KASHOG. Why should I care?

DORJE. You must teach me.

KASHOG. Go to the Buddhists in that big building at the end of the street. You can't miss it. It's about a mile long, and just as high. They'll talk you out of your desires a thousand different ways, and in no time, you'll be wandering round grinning like a cow to the slaughter.

DORJE. You teach the short path.

KASHOG. You are getting on my nerves. I may vanish you.

DORJE. I can't be any worse than I am now.

Pause.

KASHOG. I'll teach you. Go out into the street. There's a whole world out there. Women. Forget I said that. Gambling. Holy places. The Dalai Lama to bow to and beg blessings from. Drink to make you feel a king. Things to fill the mind a million to a minute. Have a bet. I enjoy a gamble. Don't use any magic to find out what's going to win. In fact, I normally lose, but I enjoy it. When you enter the world of men, go the whole hog. That's all I have to teach. Now you're keeping me from the races.

DORJE. That's not enough

KASHOG *stands up, and surveys the bucket.*

KASHOG. Shit. Look. Nothing. Now I have to carry all that shit around with me all day, and it's your fault.

DORJE. Help me. Please.

Silence.

KASHOG. What's your name?

DORJE. Dorje.

KASHOG. Listen, Dorje, would you believe me if I told you that my magic wouldn't help you.

DORJE. No.

KASHOG. I've paid good money for my share in this world, and you're keeping me from the profit of it. What can you pay me to make up for that?

DORJE. I have only my hate.

KASHOG. I'll get a lot of joy out of that. I take only precious jewels.

DORJE. That's all I have.

KASHOG. Not quite.

DORJE. What? Tell me the price. I'll give you anything. Anything.

KASHOG. This girl.

DORJE. Genyen?

KASHOG. Genyen. I bet she's a sight more interesting than the whores I've been getting lately. I'll take her, in payment. Just for one night. I bore easily.

DORJE. Keep your filthy dreams to yourself.

KASHOG. It's been nice talking to you. But if you won't sell me your mare, I have others out there, running for me. (*He starts to go.*)

DORJE. Wait!

KASHOG *stops.*

I must have revenge.

Silence.

It's some game. You ask me for the one thing I can't give. It's impossible.

KASHOG. But it's not, Dorje. Here's the bargain. I will take the one thing you desire. She's no use to you anyway, is she? I'll teach you how to give her. The demon or lover who came to you in the night had no real body. You couldn't touch her. But in every other way she lived in your mind. You made her. That's the magic I deal in. There is only the mind, Dorje. The mind creates everything. And when the mind is trained it can create in flesh and blood as well as fantasy. Do you understand what I say?

DORJE. No. But I will.

Silence.

KASHOG. It means I have to go back to the mountains. Months. Years of work. There's always some flea like you to make us itch.

Girl (*sings*).

I sought out the master with devotion
To take back the sword to my mother
My master spoke
Words became smoke
And I saw the face of another
The compassionate one has stolen my mind
I see the face of my lover.

Blackout.

Scene Eight

The mountain.
An empty space, except for DORJE *and* KASHOG. KASHOG *sits.*

DORJE. Why do you keep me waiting?

KASHOG. The mountains sometimes cool us.

DORJE. Not me.

KASHOG. No.

DORJE. Give me the teaching.

KASHOG. First things first. I haven't been paid yet. First you have to deliver Genyen to me.

DORJE. How? How can the mind make flesh and blood?

KASHOG. You will work in meditation until you see only Genyen's face behind your eyelids.

DORJE. I see only her face now.

KASHOG. But one night, when you open your eyes, she'll be standing there in front of you. And she'll be there in flesh and blood. This I promise you. Then you will call my name, and I'll take possession of your payment. I'll take her body to do with, as my imagination tells me. And I have a fearful imagination, Dorje . . . Fearful. And you will sit, and watch. And when you can't bear the sight anymore, you'll close your eyes to find us coupling behind the lids as well. For this, I will teach you how to create demons that will work for the satisfaction of your revenge.

Silence.

KASHOG. Do you believe I can do this?

DORJE. Yes.

KASHOG. And do you accept my terms?

DORJE. Yes. I must be free of this pain.

KASHOG. Fuck you. Fuck your pain.

Blackout.

Scene Nine

The disciple's space.

DORJE *sits in meditation. The light slowly fades up from darkness.* DORJE *has his eyes closed. The light gets brighter. He opens his eyes.*

DORJE. Kashog!

The light continues to build. He closes his eyes again. The light builds relentlessly to white.

Blackout.

Sudden daylighting.

KASHOG *stands behind* DORJE, *who retains his meditation position for the duration of the scene.*

KASHOG. It's morning.

DORJE. You enjoyed it.

KASHOG. Did I? (*Pause.*) Does it matter?

Silence.

DORJE. Where is she?

KASHOG. I destroyed your creation. Does it matter?

Silence.

You won't release me from my bond?

Silence. KASHOG *wipes a hand across his face; he looks old, and saddened.*

I have to give you what secrets I have. They're incomplete, Dorje. Perhaps all ways are. B
they may be enough for the satisfaction of your revenge. The demons you have to evoke ar
not known to me. They are of a form that can only be shaped by your inner desires. But the
will exist and have minds capable of dreaming of their own. How you will control these
demons and force them to your revenge is the final test. But now is the time for invocation.

Blackout.

Scene Ten

Overlooking the valley.

A bare stage.

The rhythm of the lighting as the previous scene.

In the darkness DORJE *is making the final ritual.*
It is a dance and incantation.
In his hand he holds the small drum, and in the other, the magic dagger.
He turns in a circle on the spot.
*The sounds that he makes are not audible as words. As he continues, and the light becomes a
little stronger, shapes begin to form behind him, half human, half mechanical or angular. The
form a line behind him. As he nears completion of the ritual, and the light becomes stronger,
becomes apparent they are, in fact, members of the Chinese People's Liberation Army,
carrying over their shoulders, bicycles, rifles, wireless equipment, etc.*

DORJE *completes the ritual.*

The light is at its highest.

He sees them.

DORJE. At last.

DORJE *falls on his face. They take a step forward.*

Blackout.

ACT TWO

Scene One

Outside Jamyang's house.

JAMYANG *stands, eyes closed, incanting* 'Om mani padme om' *as he counts off his prayer beads.*

DORJE's MOTHER, *bent over by the side of him, head bowed, holds up a number of white silk scarves.*
GENYEN *stands, looking down into the valley.*

JAMYANG. . . . Om mani padme om. Ooommm. Armed?

GENYEN. Lord?

JAMYANG. Armed? Are they armed?

GENYEN. Yes.

JAMYANG *groans; looks up to the sky.*

JAMYANG. O compassionate one, why me? Why my valley? I desire nothing but peace. I do not kill. I do not lust. I do not even eat meat. Lord Tserig, he eats meat! Why me? I follow the eightfold path. Why do they beat their way to my door? Why did our army not protect us? I pay the tax. Why did His Holiness make peace with them?

GENYEN. They are almost here.

JAMYANG. The scarves? Where are the scarves? (*Sees them.*) Oh. Hum. (*Mumbles*) One, two, three, four, five, six, seven, eight . . . How many are there?

GENYEN. Five.

JAMYANG. Five? Five. Good. How many rifles?

GENYEN. Only two.

JAMYANG. Only? One would be enough. Om. Om mani. Mani. What will they want? They missed Tserig. Why me? Padme. Om . . . padme . . . mani. Oh. Perhaps I should have worn my golden sword. It might have impressed them. Being a general. Do they have generals?

GENYEN. They are here.

The Chinese enter. TUNG, the radio operator, in his fifties. SHAI, the propaganda officer, a woman in her late twenties. CHANG, a teenage girl, their 'barefoot doctor'. TUNG and a YOUNG SOLDIER are armed. DORJE, dressed in Chinese clothing, follows them. They stand silent.

JAMYANG (*clearing his throat*). Hum. Hum. Hum. Welcome. (*Louder.*) Welcome. Honoured guests. (*Holds out the first scarf.*) It is the custom in our land that the –

TUNG. In your land, comrade?

JAMYANG (*putting his arm down*). In this, the Tibetan region of the . . . excellent –

TUNG. Glorious.

JAMYANG. Glorious republic of China. Yes. (*Smiles, nods at them.*)

TUNG. Yes?

JAMYANG. Yes.

Silence. He looks down and sees the scarf in his hand.

Ah, yes. It is the custom to honour distinguished guests with the gift of a white scarf of peace. Come, wife.

He steps forward, and places the scarf around the neck of TUNG. GENYEN *gives them o to the others. The Chinese remain silent.*GENYEN *goes to place one around* DORJE'*s neck and recognises him. She cries out sharply, and steps back. The scarf falls to the ground.* DORJE *does not take his eyes from* JAMYANG.

Silence, woman. She means no offence. Women. Highly strung. They see ghosts and monsters everywhere.

SHAI. Yes.

JAMYANG. Tibetan women, that is. Not all women. (*He goes to pick up the scarf.*)

SHAI. Leave it.

JAMYANG *remains kneeling.*

Let the scarf lie like a road of peace between us. And along this road will travel great changes for the people.

JAMYANG *rises, and crosses back to* GENYEN, *who has returned to* DORJE'*s* MOTHER.

TUNG. The Chairman of Our Republic, Mao Tse Tung, and the leader of the Tibetan autonomous region, the Dalai Lama, live in perfect accord. While all internal concerns are controlled by the Tibetan regional authority, we, the People's Liberation Army, are to assi the peaceful transition to a democratic society. You, as a progressive landlord, understand the need for mutual assistance?

JAMYANG. Exactly. Exactly.

TUNG. And you share your Dalai Lama's desires?

JAMYANG. I have always been most progressive.

TUNG. An example for the others –

JAMYANG. Thank you.

TUNG. Would be useful.

JAMYANG. Ah.

Silence.

SHAI. A sign of friendship.

JAMYANG. Tea? Not the filth they drink here. I have china tea.

SHAI. The old woman?

JAMYANG. Yes. Go. Get cakes.

The MOTHER *does not move.*

JAMYANG (*raising his arm*). Old fool. Are you deaf?

GENYEN. No.

He stops himself in time.

SHAI. Is she a relative?

JAMYANG (*laughing*). No. She's a serf.

SHAI. What is her name.

JAMYANG. Her name?

Silence.

SHAI. It is agreed that the evil of serfdom must be eliminated.

JAMYANG. Is it?

SHAI. You are progressive?

JAMYANG. Yes, but it takes time, surely.

TUNG. The progressive leads the way, and shows to others the right action.

JAMYANG. But what will they do if we free them? They'll just wander around, and starve without our help.

SHAI. Not if they are given lands to satisfy their needs.

JAMYANG. What? Land?

Silence.

You can't mean we give the land?

Silence. The two soldiers with rifles turn out and face the valley.

SHAI. The People's Committee will honour the purchase of the land.

JAMYANG. When? In what currency?

SHAI. We will organise the necessary papers.

Silence.

GENYEN. Free her.

JAMYANG. Hum. Yes. (*He turns away, mumbling with his beads.*)

SHAI. It was the custom in your land that all remained bowed in the presence of the aristocracy. Let her stand.

JAMYANG. Stand!

The MOTHER *does not move.*

JAMYANG. Stand. Stand, you fool. Stand.

GENYEN. She's frightened.

Silence.

GENYEN. There's nothing to be afraid of. Not any more.

The MOTHER *stands.*

CHANG. You are free. You are free, mother.

The MOTHER *looks up for the first time. She opens her mouth. She cries, silently.*

TUNG. You can go back to your home.

She goes.

SHAI. Jamyang. It is good you cast the first stone that starts the avalanche towards liberation. But there is more work to be done.

JAMYANG. More? I am not well. I wish to go indoors.

SHAI. There are to be meetings. Where the people will speak of the past injustices. Where they will learn the lesson that it was men, not gods, that put rocks on their back. It would be good for you to attend.

JAMYANG. Why me? I am only the small landlord. It is the abbot who owns the valley.

SHAI. The abbot will be there.

JAMYANG (*kneeling*). I am not well.

GENYEN. He will attend.

SHAI. I know.

The Chinese leave. DORJE *stands watching* JAMYANG.

JAMYANG. I am not well. Fetch the lamas.

DORJE *turns and goes*.

Scene Two

The village outside DORJE's *workshop*

DORJE *beats out, and cools, the heads of the hoes. His* MOTHER *brings the metal out from the forge and goes back in.* TUNG, CHANG, *and the* SOLDIER *erect posts, for a tannoy system, to replace those of the prayer flags.* SHAI *measures out seed for an old* FARMER.

SHAI (*laughing*). We don't ask you to believe what we say. Test it. It's a new seed. It will grow strong and quick. It could give you two harvests instead of one. Here. We give it to you. We do not ask for part of the harvest back. Not like the monastery. You will not carry sacks to us on harvest day. We will come to you to buy if you have a surplus.

The FARMER *takes it.*

Come for more when you have seen it work.

He goes. TONDRUP, *a young monk, watches the surveying.*

(*To* TUNG.) Another who has seen the first shoots of his neighbour's crops.

TUNG. Well, I hope the harvest is plentiful. I doubt I can take much more of this tsampa.

TONDRUP. (*to* CHANG). Are you the doctor?

CHANG. Yes. Are you ill?

TONDRUP. I have these.

He clutches a small bag around his neck.

CHANG. And do those charms keep you well?

TONDRUP. They keep the demons of sickness away.

CHANG. Always?

TUNG. Why are you not at the monastery?

TONDRUP. Not enough food. The monks I served no longer wanted me. They freed me.

TUNG. We freed you, boy.

TONDRUP. Not enough food. The serfs keep it for themselves.

TUNG. There are no serfs any more. Are you hungry?

Silence.

Give him the last of the rice.

CHANG. Have you brought your begging bowl?

TONDRUP *does not answer.* CHANG *gets a bowl of rice and offers it to him.*

Eat.

He turns and walks some way off.

Why will they not let me help them? Instead of paying the lamas to mumble over them. We should have the entire village out killing flies, with the lack of sanitation here.

TUNG. They are Buddhists. They don't kill flies.

CHANG. There's no choice, or the flies will go on killing them.

SHAI. Perhaps they should convert the flies to Buddhism. Then they wouldn't bite.

TUNG. Don't worry. The new sewage system will starve the flies out.

CHANG *is still holding the bowl.*

CHANG. Comrade! I leave the bowl here.

She places it on the ground. TONDRUP *looks away.*

If only we could make a direct challenge to the hold of the monasteries.

SHAI. Patience. Our example will win the people. It takes time to woo them from superstition. It is different from home. Only the ghosts of our ancestors haunted us there.

TUNG. As long as we are prepared when the road comes. The imperialists over the hills in India may not wait for us.

SHAI. Did it not take time in your village?

TUNG. You forget, comrade. I was on the Long March. And no villages were like these.

SHAI. He will eat. He has no choice.

TUNG. Get the boy to work.

He turns back to his surveying.

SHAI (*smiling to* CHANG). It is the thin air. It makes us irritable. He will eat. He has no choice.

The MOTHER *enters, and places the hot metal by* DORJE. SHAI *crosses to her.* CHANG *resumes work, keeping an eye on* TONDRUP.

SHAI. How is the work coming on?

MOTHER. I can't believe it, you know. Every time I get the forge going, I say, my fire. For me. And when I carry the water, I keep having to remind myself. It's for me. Not for them to bath in, and for me to carry back to their field. I keep hitting myself to make sure I'm not dreaming.

SHAI. And how are the new hoes getting on?

MOTHER. Mind you, it's backbreaking work. Somebody else to help out would be good, but I'm far from complaining. I turned my prayer wheel for many a year asking a lot less than this.

SHAI. It was a very different wheel that helped all this come about. You'll see.

MOTHER. You believe what you like. But I know.

SHAI. Wait until the road comes, mother. By then you'll have a new workshop, and your son will be at the centre of the village.

MOTHER. Will he be important?

SHAI. The worker is always important.

MOTHER. Why?

   TONDRUP *crosses over, and begins to eat.*

SHAI. Because he leads the village forward.

MOTHER. Hear that, Dorje? Leader of the village. Before only the outcasts who cut up the corpses were lower than us.

SHAI. There will be no more outcasts.

MOTHER. One son who can read, and another leads the village. I couldn't ask for anything more. If I just had a bit of help.

SHAI. We'll see what we can do.

   SHAI *watches* TONDRUP. *The* MOTHER *goes.* DORJE *beats out the next hoe,* SHAI *crosses to* TONDRUP.

   Do you want to eat regularly?

TONDRUP. Yes.

SHAI. And do you want to work?

TONDRUP (*reluctantly*). Yes.

SHAI. No one will beat you.

TONDRUP. Can I work with the doctor?

SHAI. Help the blacksmith. It's good work.

TONDRUP. Yes. (*Pause.*) Can she listen to me first?

SHAI. Who?

TONDRUP. The doctor?

CHANG. What do you want to say to me?

TONDRUP. No. I mean, listen to me. With that thing you have. I've seen you. Listening to people inside. When the lamas come they don't listen to you. They read to you. But you listen.

SHAI. He needs to be fit. The work is hard.

CHANG. Yes.

   She picks up her bag, with stethoscope, and crosses to him. SHAI *returns to measuring out grain. The* MOTHER *returns.*

SHAI. You have your help.

MOTHER. I knew you wouldn't let me down.

TONDRUP. Can you hear me?

CHANG. Yes.

TONDRUP. What am I saying?

CHANG. 'What am I saying?'

TONDRUP. Am I? (*Pause.*) Oh, yes.

   A SOLDIER *enters and whispers with* TUNG.

   Is your village like this?

CHANG. No. It is a big city.

TONDRUP. A city?

CHANG. A big town. Called Peking.

TONDRUP. Is that in China?

CHANG. Your village is in China as well.

TONDRUP. Is it?

CHANG. My town is a long way away. We can't even see the mountains.

TONDRUP. Can I go there?

CHANG. There's work to do here first.

   TUNG *crosses to* SHAI, *and talks quietly to her. The* SOLDIER *waits.*

TUNG. Jamyang sends a message. He is ill. He wishes not to attend any more re-education meetings.

DORJE (*suddenly*). He must attend the meetings. Drag him here if he can't walk.

   Silence.

SHAI. Good. The people should see the weak landlord.

CHANG. Should I go and look at him?

TUNG. We did not run to help our oppressors with precious medicines.

   The SOLDIER *leaves.* DORJE *begins his hammering again.* CHANG *turns back to* TONDRUP. *She smiles at him. He grins back.* TUNG *tunes the radio in to Chinese music. The Tibetans stand amazed.*

Scene Three

Outside the workshop.
Morning. DORJE *sits, with the upturned bike minus one wheel, in front of him.* TONDRUP, *in Chinese clothing, sits to one side, working on the wheel. He occasionally looks up at* DORJE.

TONDRUP. I can't remember how comrade Tung told us these spokes went in. (*Pause.*) It was simple the way he did it. Why should they carry bikes over the mountains, when there are no roads?

   DORJE *spins the wheel.*

TONDRUP. He just twisted something, and . . . (*Pause.*) I wish I knew what to do. Do you know, comrade? Dorje?

   DORJE *stops the wheel.*

DORJE. Why do you watch me all the time?

TONDRUP *turns away.*

You missed the meeting.

TONDRUP. I named the monks who beat me weeks ago. They've fled. To Lhasa. They can't harm me any more.

DORJE. That's not the point.

Silence.

TONDRUP. I've been sick.

DORJE. You've been traipsing after that Chinese girl. You follow her around like a lovesick cow.

TONDRUP. What would you know of love?

DORJE *looks at him.*

(*Flinching.*) I'm not well.

DORJE. The only cure is work.

TONDRUP. I'm trying to work.

DORJE. The meetings are our work. Be there.

DORJE *turns away.* TONDRUP *does not know what to do.* TASHI *enters, with his* MOTHER. DORJE *sees him.*

Have you bought your begging bowl, Tashi?

TASHI. I have come to beg. In a way.

DORJE. There is no begging now. Those who work, eat. Those too sick or old receive their share. Those who think they should be fed as they have always been – they will have to feel the pangs of hunger to bring them to their senses.

TASHI. Is that why the villagers are no longer allowed to give us offerings?

DORJE. Each man can do what he likes with his food. If he wants to cut it up for the birds, more fool him.

MOTHER (*to* TONDRUP). Leave us to talk.

TONDRUP. Yes.

DORJE. You stay here and work. You've no need to run and hide at the sight of a monk now.

TONDRUP. No (*He sits.*)

DORJE *picks up a spanner, and pretends to work on the bike.*

DORJE. What is it? Can't you see I'm busy? Is it chains again?

Silence.

TASHI. How long must these trials go on, Dorje?

DORJE. As long as it takes to make the oppressors see the error of their ways.

TASHI. But you have achieved that. They've all grovelled in front of you, even our abbot. They've given their land away, kept only a barren strip for themselves. Most of them will die over the winter.

DORJE. The people demand justice.

TASHI. Must you destroy our faith as well? The Chinese promised religious freedom. But they are starving us out. Even the richest monks can no longer afford to buy food. It won't be long before they come to melt the gold on the buddhas.

DORJE. Is your faith only in precious metals?

TASHI (*tired*). I don't know.

DORJE. What are you begging for, Tashi?

TASHI. The abbot. He is an old frightened man. All he asks is to renounce the world. To be walled up in a cave to recite his prayers. Prayers the Chinese believe do no man good, but, surely, will do them no harm.

DORJE. And did his prayer do me no harm?

TASHI. He was wrong. He should have shown mercy. But he acted only according to tradition. The tradition had lost the compassion of Buddha. I admit that. But you've smashed that tradition. That cannot happen again. Why hound the man who was only its servant?

DORJE. Not just me. There are many who still desire to speak his name, and the name of other monks.

TASHI. There were, Dorje. When you first came, there were many with grievances like you. But now the frightened imaginings of the people pile up charges higher than the mountains. They fear if they stop naming others, someone in turn may well accuse them.

DORJE. No.

MOTHER. We have all dreamt, Dorje. Now we can make something of it. We shouldn't crush the Buddha underfoot as well.

TASHI. You're blinded, brother. Is there nothing from our past that you can cherish? Not one silence from which man may draw strength, not one word of the teaching that gives a new respect and love for man? Do you want to spit on the jewel at the centre of the lotus? Will that bring you relief from your hate?

DORJE. Where were you, Tashi, when I cried for mercy? Even the mercy of the butcher's knives to kill myself. You stood by me, didn't you? You showed me this precious jewel. Don't you come to the meetings, brother, or I will cry your name out across the valley. Follow your fat friends to Lhasa and luxury, and make your trouble there. Wall your master in, but tell him always to keep an ear for the knock on the door, when the merciless come for satisfaction.

TASHI. You have such little control over your demons. That was all we tried to save you from.

DORJE. Tashi! I see you again, and that name will be upon my lips.

MOTHER. I will pray for you.

TASHI *goes.*

DORJE. There's always only snow and fire.

MOTHER. The same game over and over. You were bad enough as children. If your father had any sense and stayed alive, it might have been different. Men. I'll have to do it all myself again. (*She squats with her prayer wheel.*) How long will it take this time?

DORJE (*turning on* TONDRUP). Why are you looking at me?

TONDRUP. Don't beat me.

The MOTHER *spins her wheel and incants, inaudibly.*

Scene Four

Outside the workshop.

Early evening. As the scene progresses, darkness falls. The Chinese, with DORJE *and* TONDRUP, *clear the space of blacksmith equipment, seeds, etc. The Chinese set up measuring equipment, and string up overhead cable for lighting. The* MOTHER *watches them.*

SHAI. We'd better take down the old workshop +rst.

TUNG. Good. Dorje, bring your hammer.

SHAI. This is where you'll be sleeping mother, at the back of the new workshop.

MOTHER. With the animals?

SHAI. Of course not.

MOTHER. Imagine not having to sleep with the animals. No goats to nibble your toes.

TONDRUP. What shall I do with the wood?

TUNG. Save it. It's more precious than gold up here. We'll use it to support the roof.

SHAI. Clear everything else down to the tents. They're best all in one place until we've finished.

TONDRUP. Right.

TUNG *starts to put up the cable.*

SHAI. Is the light necessary?

TUNG. We'll have to build at night as well. They've reported snow in the Eastern province. We can't afford to be without a meeting place during the winter.

SHAI. Will we have enough fuel?

TUNG. I've radioed for more with our next supplies.

SHAI. Good.

TUNG. How can we work at night? We won't be able to see what we are doing. We'll just keep bumping into one another.

CHANG. You wait and see. We have a surprise. Magic.

TUNG. I thought you didn't believe in magic.

CHANG. We don't.

SHAI. Did they reply to our report?

TUNG. They've authorised the immediate restructuring of our meetings.

SHAI. Good.

DORJE. What meetings?

SHAI. The accusation meetings are to end, Dorje. They've done well in forcing basic democratic reforms. But now the question is what people do with their freedom. They'll n survive working their own little strips. They must be taught the advantages in working together.

DORJE. What are you saying?

SHAI. We are to have new meetings, Dorje. New lessons for the people.

DORJE. What people?

SHAI. Dorje, do you understand anything we say?

DORJE. The meetings must go on.

MOTHER. He always was a stubborn child. Comes of hitting rocks all day.

SHAI. Those meetings are finished, Dorje.

DORJE. No.

SHAI. One man's voice can't dominate the will of the people. That's the old way. You know the suffering that caused. It is time now to build anew.

DORJE. The meetings go on.

SHAI. I remember how it was in my village. I had reasons to hate the landlord. But seeking endless revenge costs the revolution valuable energy for little profit. We all have to learn that.

CHANG and TONDRUP carry equipment out. SHAI turns back to her work.

DORJE. No!

He grabs SHAI's arm. TUNG turns to watch them. The SOLDIER swings his rifle from his shoulder.

You, Chinese. You. Work for me. You said so. I brought you here.

SHAI. We came, as the army of the people, to liberate. Not to make new tyrants.

DORJE. I am the leader of this village. I am the blacksmith. There will be no work for this road unless you obey me.

TUNG. No man is indispensable, comrade. Not even the Dalai Lama.

SHAI. The revolution is a road, Dorje. You either travel it with the people, or step aside, and are left behind on the march. Each man is measured by the way he faces on that road.

She shakes her head at the SOLDIER. He re-slings his rifle.

We need to bring the generator nearer.

The Chinese leave.

MOTHER. Why does the child never listen to his mother? We could have everything and you want to spit in their faces.

She follows the Chinese.

DORJE. Demons. Why don't you obey me? I am your master. Destroy those I hate. Let me see them in front of me. I summon you Jamyang, Abbot. Where are you? I summon you.

He closes his eyes. He is shaking violently. GENYEN enters.

Let me see you. Let me see you standing in front of me. Let me see you turn to dust, and scatter in the thin air. Where are you?

He opens his eyes, and sees GENYEN who has crossed over to him. Silence.

(*Cries out.*) No. No. Demons everywhere. Burning me with desires. Go I banish you. Go.

GENYEN. No, Dorje.

She moves towards him. DORJE collapses.

DORJE. Nothing but hell for me. The demons will peck at my heart like birds on the cut-up corpse.

GENYEN *looks around, as if for help. She kneels by him.*

GENYEN. Dorje. There are no demons left. You have banished them all. Your magic has done its work. Believe me. I'm not a ghost. Look at me, Dorje. (*pause.*) All these meeting Months. I've waited for you to look at me. I've willed your eyes to search me out. But they never left Jamyang's face. You made me a ghost in the shadows there. But I'm not. Believ me. I've been frightened to come into your hate. But hate or not, you've got ... you've got to look at me. Look at me! My husband made me a slave and you make me spirit. (*Fiercely.*) You have no right to torment me like this. Look at me!

He slowly turns towards her.

What do you see? I'm not decked out in my finery. I'm not the young girl you remember. I not the face you remember. Time leaves its marks even on the mountains. We only stay the same in the picture of the mind. (*Pause.*) I wondered, in my hours of silence what your fac would grow to be. (*Silence.*) Speak to me. I can't bear any more silence.

DORJE. Genyen?

GENYEN. You can see I'm no demon, Dorje. They come in all their beauty to torment you. They don't come, frightened.

DORJE. I saw my master, and you, making love.

GENYEN. No one touches me, Dorje. No one.

He reaches out towards her face.

Yes.

He touches her.

(*Smiling.*) It's hot. I can feel the heat.

DORJE. Does it burn you as well?

GENYEN. You are the blacksmith, Dorje. The flames can burn the house, or fire the forge. Your friends speak of that.

DORJE. My friends?

GENYEN. The Chinese.

DORJE. Friends?

GENYEN. You are not the only one to have suffered, Dorje. Look at their faces. I must go. Jamyang is sick. He spends what little money he has left on lamas. As long as the people obeyed him, he was strong, but in himself there were only ashes and a little smoke.

DORJE. Do you have children?

GENYEN. No.

Silence.

I must go.

DORJE. Why? Will he beat you?

GENYEN. That's all over, Dorje. You've brought a new time with you. (*Smiling.*) You stan in the middle of it, and you don't understand.

DORJE. Why are you smiling?

TONDRUP *enters.*

GENYEN. Your friends are coming back.

DORJE *sees* TONDRUP, *who stands looking at them.*

I must go.

She goes. DORJE *watches her.*

The sound of a generator starting up. DORJE *is startled. The others return in the darkness.*

MOTHER (*entering*). What is that terrible noise?

CHANG. It's a Chinese dragon waking up.

MOTHER. Well, if it starts belching smoke, I'm going.

CHANG. I thought you'd be used to that.

MOTHER. Not dragon's smoke, I'm not. And I never want to be.

TUNG *fits a light bulb into a hanging socket. The generator levels off and the bulb comes slowly to life. Silence. The Chinese watch the Tibetans with evident pleasure.*

TONDRUP. It is magic.

SHAI. It's only magic because you don't understand it. But there's no mystery. We'll explain it to you.

DORJE *crosses past them, and stares at the bulb.*

Silence.

DORJE. Where's the flame? There's nothing burning.

TUNG. That's right.

DORJE. But you can't have a candle that doesn't burn.

TUNG. In the new world you can, Dorje. You are looking at it.

DORJE. How? How can you do this?

SHAI. It's not just a trick to astonish you, Dorje. It's a tool called electricity. It can make light and heat and the strongest steel. And with it we can build machines that change all our lives. Like the tractor that will come and dig over all the valley in only a few days, with only one man to guide it.

TONDRUP. What's a tractor?

CHANG. It's like a hundred yaks on wheels.

MOTHER. That I want to live to see.

CHANG. You'll see even stranger things than that.

DORJE. And can you control this power?

SHAI. The people can. It's only one of many new tools. And with them, we can increase the harvest that people can live without fear of hunger. If only we work together.

DORJE. How does it work?

SHAI. First we must build the workshop and then we can talk of these things in the meetings.

Silence.

MOTHER. I'm getting little coloured dots in front of my eyes.

TUNG. It's not mean to be looked at. Like a jewelled statue. It has a use. Where are the pick-axes? And the shovels?

Silence.

DORJE. I will fetch them.

TUNG. Thank you, comrade.

DORJE *goes. They begin work.*

Scene Five

Inside the workshop.

Winter.

A bench. Electric work light. DORJE *is fixing the wheel on the bike.* TONDRUP *stands watching him.*

DORJE. Spanner.

TONDRUP *hands him the spanner.* DORJE *tightens the nut.*

DORJE. There.

He spins the wheel.

See?

TONDRUP *nods.*

Right. (*He undoes the wheel and takes it off.*) Now you try.

He stands back. TONDRUP *attempts to put the wheel back on.*

No.

TONDRUP. What?

DORJE. The washer. The washer goes on before the nut, or you'll bite into the frame.

TONDRUP. Yes.

As he unscrews the nut, he drops the spanner. DORJE *picks it up and hands it back to him.*

DORJE. What's the matter, Tondrup?

TONDRUP. Nothing.

DORJE. You've been like it for days. Do you want to talk?

TONDRUP. I'm not well.

DORJE. Well, you spend enough time with the doctor. Hasn't she told you what's wrong?

TONDRUP. I'm not sleeping well, that's all.

DORJE. What does Chang say about that?

TONDRUP. I haven't told her.

DORJE. Why not?

TONDRUP *turns back to the bike.*

Is she part of it? Part of the bad dreams?

TONDRUP. What bad dreams?

DORJE. We sleep in the same room, Tondrup.

TONDRUP (*pauses*). I don't know what they are. I don't know what they mean. I never had them in the monastery. I respect her, I do. When I see her now, the dreams are there. I try to stop them coming when I look at her, but . . . I don't know what's happening to me.

DORJE. Are they so bad?

TONDRUP. You wouldn't understand.

Silence.

DORJE. Let's see if we can put the chain on. When the road comes we must know everything there is to know about this bike. There will be big machines to work on then. And when the snow goes, we must go out to the small villages and talk to them of the changes that are coming. Do you dream about that, Tondrup? Do you dream what our world could be like?

TONDRUP. Sometimes.

DORJE. Hook it over the small one first.

TONDRUP. Yes.

DORJE. Does she love you?

TONDRUP. I don't know. Yes. I think so.

DORJE. Do you think she has bad dreams as well?

TONDRUP. No. Of course not.

DORJE. How do you know?

Silence.

Do you think that what you desire is really evil?

TONDRUP. At the monastery they would have beaten me for what I'm feeling now.

DORJE. But it wouldn't have gone away, you know. The monks had no way of destroying it.

TONDRUP. Then am I evil?

DORJE. You are no different from the rest of us.

TONDRUP. But I can't work. Not like you. Not with these dreams.

DORJE. You need dreams to work. If we kill them we work like serfs, like donkeys. They are not sinful. They are our hope. Our energy. They are what makes us want to build a better world.

He has fixed the chain on.

DORJE. There.

TONDRUP. I can never do it.

DORJE. Take the whole bike to bits.

TONDRUP. What?

DORJE. Take the bike to bits, and then put it together again.

TONDRUP. I can't.

DORJE. Work it out. Talk to her. You may be surprised. Anything's possible, Tondrup. That's what the Liberation Army has brought to us. But we have to work it out.

TONDRUP *begins to strip the bike down.*

Scene Six

The street.

The sound of the radio receiver. Lights. Chinese have set up a propaganda table. TUNG with headphones on is writing down a report. The other Chinese stand around the table. TUNG takes off the headphones.

SHAI. Well?

TUNG. The reactionaries have begun their last game. Demonstrations in the street. Lhasa could explode at any moment. We are to maintain an open radio channel at all times.

SHAI. What of the Dalai Lama?

TUNG. No news. He's still locked in the summer palace. The army has taken no action as yet. Except in cordoning the city off. Every class traitor in Tibet has willingly trapped himself there. And it must be contained there. The villages must hear nothing of this until it is suppressed.

SHAI. Of course.

TUNG. Do you understand, Chang?

CHANG. I won't tell anybody.

TUNG. Our primary task is to keep the road moving. It's less than a week away now, and we must press on even faster than before. The imperialists might well try to exploit any internal weaknesses, so the border road is critical. We are to prepare contingency plans for an increased labour force in the event of a National Emergency. They are going to play right into our hands. We've waited long enough.

DORJE and his MOTHER and TONDRUP arrive, with a bike.

TUNG. A delegation.

DORJE. Greetings, comrades.

SHAI. Greetings.

DORJE. We come to return your bike. Can you check the tyres, please? Are they too hard?

SHAI *checks them.*

SHAI. The tyres are fine.

DORJE. Tondrup. Ask that question?

TONDRUP (*indicates the lamp placement*). What is this for?

SHAI. That is where you put the light.

TONDRUP. Like the light in the workshop?

SHAI. Similar.

TONDRUP. But how do you ride with all the wires?

SHAI. There are no wires.

DORJE. Like the wireless?

SHAI. Exactly, they run off batteries.

TONDRUP. And do you have one of these lights?

SHAI. No. They are not being made yet. But one day.

DORJE. So we prepare the bike for something that does not exist yet.

SHAI. Yes. The same as we prepare your training in advance for a road that is not yet here.

DORJE. Do you understand now?

TONDRUP. Yes. Well . . .

SHAI. But why have you returned the bike?

DORJE. Because now we know what makes the wheels turn.

MOTHER. They've taken it to bits and put it back together a thousand times over these last months. We'll be the best workshop from here to Lhasa.

SHAI. Do you know everything about that bike?

TONDRUP. We do. Well, Dorje does.

The radio receiver starts up. TUNG *goes to answer it.*

SHAI (*mock serious*). Don't look so proud. I believe there's something you don't know.

MOTHER. There's nothing my son doesn't know.

DORJE. Mother.

SHAI. Can he ride it?

MOTHER. Ride it?

SHAI. You don't know a bike until you can ride it.

MOTHER. All those years of being a blacksmith and we never rode a horse.

SHAI. But you never owned a horse. Things have changed. He owns a bike now.

DORJE. I don't own a bike. It's your bike.

SHAI. No. It's owned by the one with the greatest need. It's you who'll be going up and down the road, telling the people of land reform; persuading them that tractors and trucks are not fire-eating demons. We only came to teach. When you can do that yourself, we must find other work. Perhaps they will send me back to my own village. It's warmer there.

DORJE. Is your family there?

SHAI. My parents, and brothers.

MOTHER. And a husband?

SHAI. No. Now, Dorje. Get on the saddle.

DORJE. What, here? Where everyone can see me?

SHAI. We learn in public. Not in private. Besides, others will learn from your mistakes. It is not a bad way of teaching.

Under SHAI's *instructions, and to the amusement of his friends,* DORJE *attempts to ride the bike.*

SHAI. On the saddle. Shift your leg over. Good. Both feet on the pedals. I've got you. (DORJE *falls off.*) Pick it up. You're quite safe. When I push, you pedal. Ready? There. Use the handlebars to steer. Your front wheel's your guiding wheel. You're on your own.

TUNG *switches off the receiver and crosses to* SHAI.

TUNG. A word, Shai.

SHAI. You're doing well. Just keep practising.

TONDRUP (*to* CHANG). Will I get a bike one day?

CHANG. Of course. And a light.

TUNG (*to* TONDRUP). Go and help your friend. Chang!

TONDRUP *crosses back to* DORJE. CHANG *and* TUNG *return to the group.*

TONDRUP. Can I have a go?

DORJE. Let me get the hang of it, and then we'll share it.

MOTHER. It doesn't look as nice as a horse.

DORJE. It's cheaper to feed.

MOTHER. No dung though, is there?

DORJE. You can't have everything. Look, Shai, I think I've almost got it.

He manages a wobbly circuit, almost running into the Chinese group who are involved in very serious, whispered conversation.

DORJE. What's the matter?

SHAI (*to* TUNG). We'll have to make an announcement.

TUNG. This is now security. Propaganda will have to wait until we're prepared.

DORJE. What is it? You must tell me.

TUNG (*to* CHANG). You must treat no more patients. We may need all the supplies we can get.

SHAI. Your people have been too slow, Dorje.

DORJE. My people?

TUNG. You Tibetans must wake up to the fact that the rest of China can't wait for you. You live in dreams. We'll move into the workshop. It is the only solid base until support comes. Then we can go up to the monastery.

SHAI. Dorje, we have to take over your shop.

DORJE. But what about our work?

SHAI. It'll have to wait. Move all your equipment, immediately.

TONDRUP. What's happening?

CHANG. Nothing. Don't worry.

TONDRUP. Why are you packing up?

SHAI. I'm sorry, Dorje.

TUNG. You're sorry. I'm sorry we ever set eyes on these crazy people. They smile, and then betray you.

DORJE. How have we betrayed you?

TUNG (*to* SURVEYORS). Get *our* people together for a meeting.

SHAI. You must understand, Dorje. We have fought a long time for our revolution. Nothing must stand in its way now.

DORJE. What have we done?

TUNG. An announcement will be made.

DORJE. Will the road stop?

TUNG. No. It will move even faster. And you Tibetans will work even harder.

The Chinese leave.
The Tibetans remain.

Scene Seven

The street.

TUNG *makes the following speech on the tannoy system.*

TUNG. On March 10th, 1959, His Holiness the Dalai Lama was invited as an honoured guest to a theatrical performance at the Military Garrison in Lhasa, by the Political Commissar, T'an Kuan-san.

However, reactionary elements of rebels and monks secretly armed by Western imperialists, alarmed the people with the fantastic rumour of a Chinese plot to kidnap the Dalai Lama. They incited the people to acts of violence. A Tibetan member of the Communist Party was stoned to death in the streets. The People's Liberation Army in no way retaliated to this crime, hoping that the crowd would come to their senses. This act of mercy was seized on by the reactionaries as a sign of weakness, and they agitated in armed demonstrations for a return to the feudal system prevailing before the Liberation.

Poisoned by the advice of highly placed monks, the Dalai Lama secretly fled Lhasa for India leaving the people without the one man who should, as political head, have brought them to their senses. Acts of terrorism increased.

On the 17th, the Army, already under extreme provocation, was asked to take action by your Panchen Lama, now the legal head of the Region.

All reactionary elements in the city have now been suppressed.

Scene Eight.

The workshop.

Electric light. Portrait of Mao. A soldier strips down his rifle on the workbench. A RADIO OPERATOR, TUNG *and* SHAI *study the map.*

TUNG. The road must reach the Western borders within two years. If we had built it already those reactionaries would not have made it so easily to India. We were far too slow.

SHAI. It's over three thousand kilometres long.

TUNG. And hardly ever below three thousand metres. It makes the Great Wall look easy. But we can do it, comrade, because we have to do it.

SHAI (*pauses*). We must avoid the difficulty we met with the first collection for the road building team or we'll lose even more of them to the hills.

TUNG. Which is why Dorje and the local leaders must head the recruiting, at least until our relief troops arrive.

SHAI. It becomes more difficult. The first list were all clearly reactionary.

TUNG. Comrade, the road is always rocky. It is our task to clear it for those who follow.

DORJE *and* TONDRUP *enter.*

TONDRUP. Will you ask them?

DORJE. Don't get so excited.

TONDRUP. Why not?

TUNG. Dorje.

DORJE. Yes, comrade.

TUNG. You are to take responsibility for the recruitment of roadworkers.

SHAI. There are far too many rumours flying around since the uprising. It is important the people are reminded of the unity between local leaders and the Liberation Army.

DORJE (*pauses*). The people talk of shootings when the reactionaries were brought in.

TUNG. Your people are easily misled.

SHAI. You see why a local man is necessary.

DORJE. Yes.

TUNG. Here is the new list.

He hands it to him.

Tondrup!

TONDRUP. Yes, master?

TUNG. Comrade.

TONDRUP. Comrade.

TUNG. We are pleased that there are some Tibetans who are not haunted by ghosts and demons. You work hard, and learn quickly.

TONDRUP. Thank you.

TUNG. It is the party's decision that you should be encouraged to use your talents to the full for our people. Within a few weeks, with the increased effort, the road will reach us. You will leave on the first outgoing convoy to study technology in the Peking Minorities College. This is a great honour and responsibility for you. But we are confident that you will richly repay it.

TONDRUP (*confused*). Leave the village?

SHAI. It's a great opportunity, Tondrup.

TONDRUP. Dorje?

DORJE. But we'll need his skills when the road comes.

TUNG. We plan further ahead than that, Dorje. Besides there'll soon be plenty of trained troops. They're to garrison in the monastery. It's part of your new duties to see that objective is achieved smoothly.

DORJE. That's why these are largely the names of monks.

Silence.

SHAI. Are you not excited?

TONDRUP. Yes, but ...

TUNG. Well?

TONDRUP. Will Chang be going back?

SHAI. The needs of the people must outweigh personal considerations.

TONDRUP. Yes. Thank you.

TUNG. Until the convoy goes, accompany Dorje on his new duties. And report back to us daily on what you have learnt.

SHAI (*smiling*). It is a great honour.

TONDRUP. Thank you.

DORJE. I'll explain to them. Don't worry.

TONDRUP *goes*.

TUNG. Anyone to add to the list?

DORJE. This has the names of women on it.

TUNG. Women can be reactionaries, just like men.

DORJE (*with difficulty*). The people are still shocked by what happened in Lhasa. Now the new restrictions. They are confused. Frightened.

TUNG. Why should they fear freedom?

DORJE. It takes some getting used to. Like you got dizzy with the thin air here. The road must be built. We have been cut off too long from the real world. But it's important that we understand. If we don't understand we are slaves again. Is that not right?

SHAI. What do you suggest, Dorje?

DORJE. Let me talk to these people. Get them to volunteer freely. They will if they understand.

TUNG. We have no more time to give you Tibetans.

DORJE. They think you have come to steal everything from them. Their belief, their religion, the Dalai Lama.

TUNG (*crosses to* RADIO OPERATOR). We tried not to interfere with the religious power of the Dalai Lama. But he wanted to keep his feudal power. All your oppression stemmed from that. Religion keeps people so drugged they don't wake up and fight back. You must have heard Shai say this a thousand times. Have you understood?

DORJE. Yes.

TUNG. Well, it is a pity the rest of your people haven't.

DORJE. They just need reassuring that there's something they can use from their past. How will they know who they are, if they keep nothing?

TUNG. You are the one who wanted to burn it all. When the mattress is infected with lice, you can't save the straw.

DORJE. Do we have nothing that we can give the revolution to help it grow?

TUNG. Only your labour.

Silence.

SHAI. Let him have a day or two. (*Aside.*) We don't have the troops yet to enforce the order, if they resist.

TUNG (*pauses*). Good. We have to relieve the supply troops.

TUNG *leaves, signalling the* SOLDIER *to join him.* SHAI *looks at* DORJE.

DORJE (*eventually*). Thank you. People are very frightened.

SHAI. Are you?

DORJE. People have to have the desire . . . the vision. Then they work. What work is it if the don't dream?

Silence. He fiddles with tools in the workshop.

I'd like to do some simple work again.

SHAI. Give it time.

DORJE. About Tondrup. And Chang. I know what you say about the needs of the people, bu they're talking of marriage.

Silence.

If we could make a bridge, a ritual, between our peoples. A wedding. We have lively weddings. Songs, dancing. Everyone drunk. And we could give your bride presents that would be useful in her home. (*Half smiling.*) Some presents aren't useful. But they give jo for the moment, like a song. And the people would see their lives valued a little. So you se he's more useful staying here.

SHAI. We *knew* about the wedding idea.

DORJE. What?

SHAI. There can be no wedding.

Silence.

DORJE. You are sending the boy away from his own home because of her. But why? You can't really think he's dangerous to her. That he'll harm her. (*Pause.*) Is that why you acce nothing from us? You fear we'll poison you in some way? You can't free us if you fear us. Fear can't free anyone. (*Pause.*) No. No. I must be wrong. I mean, you and me, we're friends. We have a bridge that we can cross. No. If I was right, they'd stop our relationship as they stopped theirs. Wouldn't they?

He looks at her. She turns away.

No. They don't need to stop our relationship. There's nothing to stop, is there? I can't give you anything. I can't give you joy, a child. I can't infect you.

SHAI. Dorje, don't go back on what you've been taught. You're just coming out of a child's world of emotion.

DORJE. You hate us. We are not human to you. What do you see when you look at our faces? What demons are we?

SHAI. Dorje. Calm down. Think. We have given you power. Don't throw it away. Just do as we say. Then you might understand.

Blackout.

Scene Nine

Genyen's strip of land.

GENYEN *works, clearing the stone from her field.* JAMYANG's *body lies in the field.* DORJE *enters, with* TONDRUP.

DORJE. Go down to the village.

TONDRUP. They said I was to go everywhere with you.

DORJE. Do as I say.

TONDRUP *goes*. DORJE *crosses to* GENYEN.

GENYEN. How many killed in Lhasa?

DORJE. I don't know. They say thousands.

GENYEN. I can't imagine so many faces. Will the tractors turn over even this rock? I don't know what to do with Jamyang's body.

DORJE. Why did he wait until the soldiers came to run? The hills are full of people following the Dalai Lama to India. Did they shoot him?

GENYEN. He collapsed, he asked for a guide to take him through into rebirth.

DORJE. The Chinese have banned all religious ceremonies. No lama would dare to do the Bardo now.

GENYEN. We should give him the chance to be born with a new understanding.

DORJE. Bury him. Forget him. We must look after ourselves now.

GENYEN. It's not impossible.

DORJE. No lama will do it.

GENYEN. Ask your brother.

DORJE. Tashi? How can I ask Tashi? He's in Lhasa.

Silence.

Where is he?

GENYEN. Hiding in the monastery, collecting food for a group he's taking through the hills.

DORJE. Where is he getting food from?

GENYEN. Everyone in the village.

DORJE. Why was I not told?

She looks at him.

I'm no traitor. It's the Chinese. They've betrayed me. They talk of one road, and take another. Tashi. We must go with Tashi. Collect your food. Tonight we go into the hills.

GENYEN. What?

DORJE. Genyen, we can't stay here. Your name is high on the road list. Are you listening? You could die on that road.

Silence.

They are watching me. All our names will be on there soon. We have to leave now.

GENYEN. This is my land. I've worked for the harvest. I want to see the tractor turn the earth.

DORJE. What are you talking about?

GENYEN. Jamyang wasn't running anywhere, Dorje. He was just running away.

DORJE. Listen to me. They are going to work us to death.

GENYEN. You talked in the meetings. I watched your face. When you talked about freedom from tyranny. Where men were equal. The Liberation Army freed you from oppression. They freed me, and Jamyang, from being oppressors. I want that world you talked about, and I want it here, in my land. And I'll work for it for as many lifetimes as it takes. I want to be reborn here.

DORJE. Look, I won't wait. There is no time. I'll go with Tashi. I'll leave you. You have to come with me.

GENYEN. Ask Tashi to give Jamyang the Bardo.

She begins work again.

DORJE. Genyen!

She does not look up. DORJE *exits.*

Scene Ten

The monastery.

The wheel of life mandala remains. DORJE *enters, and crosses to stand looking at it. His* MOTHER *enters from the other side and stands watching him.* DORJE *does not turn around.*

DORJE. Where is he?

MOTHER. Who? I just come here to pray in peace.

DORJE. Even my mother lies to me. Where's my brother?

TASHI *enters, carrying a rifle.*

TASHI. What do you want?

DORJE *turns to him.*

It is a gift from our Chinese brothers.

DORJE. Do you know how to use it?

TASHI. The Tibetan is a good pupil. Where are your masters, Dorje? They have already take mine. Could they not just have left him to starve?

Silence.

And now you have brought them for me. As you promised. Where are they? Hiding behind rocks, waiting to pick us off as we leave?

DORJE. I brought you food.

TASHI. What?

MOTHER. Take it. It is an offering.

TASHI. I came once with my begging bowl. No.

DORJE. You must leave tonight. The Chinese intend to garrison here.

TASHI. What trap is this? Don't tell me my brother has had a change of heart. Thinking of his family's welfare.

DORJE. Are you going, mother?

MOTHER. Yes.

DORJE. You were so happy. You had everything you had ever dreamt of.

MOTHER. In this life, yes. But I'm old woman. If the Dalai Lama has left, what hope is there for me in Tibet for the next life? You have to weigh one thing against another. That's good business, Dorje.

TASHI. The Dalai Lama is Tibet. Where he goes Tibet is.

DORJE. Even in India?

TASHI. The teachings came from there. The wheel has simply turned full circle.

DORJE. What do you hope for then?

TASHI. Just to keep the teaching alive. That's all.

DORJE. With a rifle?

TASHI. If that's the only way.

Silence.

DORJE. What happened in Lhasa?

TASHI. Why do you want to know?

DORJE. There's no Chinese with me, Tashi. Believe me. I left them in the valley. And I don't know whether to go back or up in the hills. Tell me about Lhasa.

Silence.

MOTHER. Speak to your brother.

TASHI. It's difficult to say clearly. There were months of rumours. Stories of atrocities told by refugee families from the east. Of monks tortured by soldiers. Then we heard that the Chinese were going to kidnap his Holiness. We were all terrified. People ran in the streets, demanding the Army went back to China. The Chinese did not react. All the women held a mass demonstration. The Chinese just watched from the housetops. Then the Dalai Lama disappeared from the summer palace. We thought they had taken him. Well, they hadn't. He'd fled. He had to. But nobody knew what was happening. Everything went mad. The people howled at the loss. The Chinese appeared on the streets. Arms sprang from everywhere. Butchers' knives. Old hunting guns. Against machine guns. Cannons. Tanks. They bombed the summer palace. They must have thought his Holiness was still there. They burnt the Cathedral. Everywhere was burning. The sacred circle around the city became mud under the boots of Chinese troops. We fought back as best we could against trained men, and were massacred in the sacred streets. They wanted to kill all of us, Dorje. All of us. Women. Children. Bleeding in the streets. Monks picking up rifles they didn't know how to hold, let alone fire. Picking up the Chinese magic, and dying with their first touch of it. Those of us left fought our way out of the city. I killed a man. I think. I'm not sure. He almost walked into me coming around a corner. He fell down. He didn't move.

Silence.

You remember your first sight of Lhasa. No one ever forgets it. The sun on the golden rooftops of the cathedral and Potala. When I left, you could see nothing but smoke and fire. they are melting down the gold of Tibet.

Silence.

MOTHER. Come with us, Dorje. Let the family be together again.

TASHI. You can't serve these masters. And you can't walk hand in hand with them. His Holiness tried that.

DORJE. They did free us. They did show us the way out of tyranny.

TASHI. Only to make you kneel under its foot again.

DORJE. I saw something. Genyen spoke of it when I tried to persuade her to leave.

TASHI. There is nothing to keep you here, Dorje. They blinded you, but you can't believe in these demons now.

DORJE. That's how they see us, you know.

TASHI. Come back to the old belief. We can keep it alive, somehow.

DORJE. Jamyang is dead. His last wish was for the Bardo to be said over him.

TASHI. There are many dead. We have to think of the living now.

DORJE. Will you read over him?

TASHI (*pauses*). Is this a game, Dorje? Some sophisticated snare to trap me in?

DORJE. Do you believe in the teaching?

TASHI. Why would you want to give the Bardo to your worst enemy?

DORJE. I don't know. At the end, he prayed for someone to guide him back to a new understanding. That's something. There was still a desire there. Not to be born the same. Not to make the same mistakes. To grow.

TASHI. You don't even believe in the teaching.

DORJE. I don't know. He did. He desired it. Can't we turn our desires into reality? Can't we follow them along the path and see where they lead?

TASHI. That is against the teaching.

DORJE. Will you do it?

TASHI. No. My responsibility is to the people I'm guiding. There's nothing to be done. The time for that is past. (*Angrily.*) And you were one of those that made that so.

DORJE. I'd do it myself, but I don't know the words. You monks kept that knowledge to yourselves.

TASHI. You're mad, Dorje. When will you ever learn?

DORJE. I'll do it. I'll cut the body, and do what rites I can.

MOTHER. You can't cut the body. That's for outcasts. We were never that low.

DORJE. (*laughing*). Mother. It's honest work. That's something the Chinese have taught me

TASHI. You have not the authority to perform the rite. It will be meaningless.

MOTHER. The Chinese won't understand. They won't let you be leader of the village. Be sensible. Come with us.

TASHI. So you still want to spit on the jewel at the centre of the lotus, after all.

Silence.

DORJE. Travel light across the mountains. The heavy snows will be here soon.

TASHI. We have responsibility. We have to carry what we can of these precious relics.

DORJE. Don't hoard the images, or you may not make it. What does it matter if the Chinese melt down the face of Buddha? You carry the image of him firmly in your minds. You can create him anywhere.

MOTHER. I will pray for you.

She goes. TASHI *turns to follow.*

TASHI *goes.*

Scene Eleven.

The hill.

A bare stage.

DORJE *drags on the body of* JAMYANG. *He lays the body down. By its side, he sets out his working knives. He sits behind the body in meditation, his eyes closed. Occasionally, he makes movements reminiscent of his 'magic' dance, but more improvised, uncertain.*

DORJE. Jamyang. I call you. Out of the rocks. Out of the air. Don't fear. Let me see your face. Yes. Turn. Please. I beg you. Look at me. Let me see your face. Yes. You can't come back to this body, Jamyang. You can't haunt this hill. Here was only suffering. Go on. There's nothing to fear about rebirth. You can't stay in the light of Buddha. There's still so many things to be done. Rebirth is your hope. Not to pay for past sins, serving time. No. Serving man. Tending the soil. Helping the earth flower. There's no need of suffering in that. Don't take the new world as you find it – it's yours to shape and share. Don't turn to the shadows. (*Cries out.*) No. See through them, Jamyang. Those demons that taunt you now, have no substance. They haunted you in your last life, in your dark. They are not your masters. You made them. You brought them into being. Deny them flesh and blood. There's only the mind. Find the hope. Let that set the pattern for rebirth. Find the wish. Wish. Wish. Wish. Let the demons fade away. See through them as the smoke clears. See through them as the clouds part. Search only for the earth where you will work. See how beautiful it is. The blue of the seas. See the patterns of mountains and valleys. See the cities and small villages. Search. See the people. Look for someone else other than your own face in the mirror. See the face of the woman. The face of the man. See them lie down on the rags, in the light of the oil lamp. Share their joining together, their sweat, their violence, their pain, their joy, their work, their love. Don't close your eyes. You who made love in the dark. Face it. What is there here that we need to lock ourselves away from? They have told you to fear life itself, and seek escape. What is there here to fear? Watch them. You are part of them. Part of their loins. Part of their life. Part of the creation. Don't fight them. Enter their ecstasy. Give up your old shame. Give up your old name. It's time to return. Time for the seed at the centre of it. Let go the past. Go. Join them. Unite them. The seed. Change.

He cries out. His posture relaxes. He laughs quietly. CHINESE SOLDIERS *have entered and stand watching him. He opens his eyes. He sees them. He reaches slowly for one of his butcher's knives. They raise their rifles.*

I have to cut up the body for the birds, so he can't come back as the landlord again.

He starts to cut up the body. The SOLDIERS *step forward. Sound effect of generators.*

Scene Twelve

The road.

Deafening roar of generators. Light from powerful arc lamps cuts the stage.

Chinese armed GUARDS, *faces covered with scarves against the dust, stand over similarly muffled Tibetans. It is impossible to discern individual faces, only among the Tibetans are at least one woman and a monk. They carry rocks and shale into the centre of the road, where others smash them into smaller pieces before the surfacing begins. All the Tibetans are obviously exhausted.* TUNG *enters with* SHAI *and* CHANG. *They watch the work. He checks his watch and the light beyond the arc lights. He signals for the arc lights to be switched off. The generators cease. A moment's silence. The Tibetans sit, some lie down, in the moment's respite.*

CHANG *checks over the fallen figure of a Tibetan.*

TUNG. Will he make the double shift?

CHANG. Yes.

As SHAI *begins to read,* GENYEN *takes off her scarf, and wipes her face with it. An old Tibetan begins building a small cairn with the stones.*

SHAI (*reading*). The mistakes of the past must be exposed without sparing anyone's sensibilities; we must analyse and criticise what was bad in the past with a scientific attitude so that work in the future will be done more carefully and better. This is what is meant by 'Learn from the past mistakes and avoid future ones'. But our aim in exposing errors is like that of a doctor curing a sickness. It is solely to save the patient and not to doctor him to death. So long as a patient does not hide his sickness for fear of treatment or persist in his mistakes until he is beyond cure, so long as he honestly and sincerely wishes to be cured and to mend his ways, we should welcome and cure his sickness so that he can become a good comrade. In treating an ideological or a political malady one must never be rough or rash but must adopt the approach of 'curing the sickness to save the patient'.

Silence.

Who will be the first to speak, to share his self-criticism and new understanding?

DORJE *stands. As he speaks, and daylight becomes stronger, the houselights slowly come up.*

DORJE. I criticise myself for my past and present mistakes, and failures in truly working for the revolution. I am sick, and I ask my comrades to help work with me for the cure. My main mistake is a failure to question and understand. I work on the road but I work like a donkey, not like a man. My mind is full of dreams. I do not ask myself all the time, who is this road for? Why have we decided to build it? Is it for the people? Who are the people? Where is this road going? I should ask these questions more often, and out loud, so that my comrades can help me in answering them.

He looks at the other Tibetans, including GENYEN, *and then turns back to* SHAI. SHAI *looks at* TUNG.

Blackout.